Social Value in Public Policy

Bill Jordan

Social Value in Public Policy

palgrave
macmillan

Bill Jordan
University of Plymouth
Exeter, UK

ISBN 978-3-030-60420-2 ISBN 978-3-030-60421-9 (eBook)
https://doi.org/10.1007/978-3-030-60421-9

This Palgrave Macmillan imprint is published by the registered company Springer Nature Switzerland AG.
The registered company address is: Gewerbestrasse 11, 6330 Cham, Switzerland

To the memory of Jean Packman, partner, colleague and inspiration

Acknowledgements

For helpful discussions and suggestions, I would like to thank Sarah Jordan, Henry Jordan, Simon Pearson, Linda and Colin Janus-Harris, Alexandra Allan and John Ingham.

Contents

CHAPTER 1

Introduction

Abstract Social value is created in human interactions, and is the basis for our well-being. But these interactions are influenced by the policies of governments, and hence well-being can often be undermined by them. This book will consider how such policies, which reduce the levels of social value accumulated in economies and societies, could be minimised, and how relationships which enhance social value (and hence well-being) could be strengthened and enhanced. The coronavirus pandemic has greatly re-enforced longstanding tendencies in US and UK societies, and caused a dramatic collapse in national income and in well-being, but it also supplies an opportunity to re-assess social policies across the board.

Keywords Relationships • Services • Well-being • Inequality

The recession caused by the coronavirus lock-down had especially severe effects on face-to-face activities – those which could accelerate the pandemic's spread. Services of this kind had been forming an ever-growing proportion of employment in advanced economies, especially the USA and UK. In the latter in March, 2018, there were almost 33 million workers in services of all kinds, almost five and a half million of whom were (despite programmes of privatisation) in the public sector, out of a total labour force of some 40 million. Around a million workers in all were

B. Jordan, *Social Value in Public Policy*,
https://doi.org/10.1007/978-3-030-60421-9_1

immediately laid off in the pandemic, and some of their employers faced bankruptcy.

The dominance of service employment in these economies dated from the 1960s, when industrial production started to be relocated to the Far East and South America; by 1980, this had been identified as the 'globalisation' of economic activity, with China's rapid growth as its totem phenomenon. But the other obvious consequence of the market-minded public policies which became the orthodoxies under Margaret Thatcher's and Ronald Reagan's leaderships was a growing inequality of earnings in the populations of the two nations.

Both countries' governments (under their respective major parties' regimes) had opted to offset the very low wages which characterised much service employment, especially in the private sector, with subsidies from the public purse. In the first 20 years of their expanded coverage in the UK (and Ireland, where they still are) these were called Family Income Supplements; at the end of the century, a Labour government adopted their US name of Tax Credits, recognising that they worked as a kind of income tax in reverse, and in this century the UK's were renamed 'Universal Credit' (UC).

Face-to-face services were also important factors in an approach to assessing the *quality* of life in our societies which became prominent at the turn of the century (Kahneman 1999; Helliwell 2003; Layard 2005). Here the concept of Subjective Well-being (SWB), which could be measured through mass surveys, allowed comparisons to be made between genders, classes, marital statuses, occupations, age groups, districts and so on. But it was also possible to make international comparisons, and to determine which policies and social trends (e.g. spending on public services, and rates of family breakdown) increased SWB, and which reduced it.

The striking finding about these statistical comparisons, especially in the USA and UK, was that average SWB had not risen in the decades since the 1970s, when its measurement was first systematically recorded. This had provoked animated debates among economists, psychologists, political scientists and sociologists, about the nature and causes of this stagnation in levels of happiness, since scores for SWB in developing countries continued to rise as their economies were growing.

Part of the explanation clearly lay in the rise in inequality, especially in the Anglophone countries; more equal societies, such as the Scandinavian ones, did better (Wilkinson and Pickett 2009). But the least happy of all in all types of society were poor people forced to take low-paid work (or to work longer hours in such jobs) on pain of losing all or part of their benefits or state subsidies to their wages (Haagh 2019). This applied even to beneficiaries in Sweden, one of the most equal societies with the highest average levels of SWB; 'workfare' participants there were no more contented than the citizens of Brazil or Turkey.

So it matters *how* incomes are redistributed as well as how much. A large part of the reason for this was revealed by studies of the components of SWB. Ill health and long-term disability were the largest factors reducing levels below the average, but all kinds of relationships were the main components in well-being and unhappiness – more significant than income levels. Divorce and separation, widowhood and unemployment were leading negative factors.

This suggested that SWB itself was strongly influenced by the quality of relationships, and that interpersonal transactions, both formal and informal, contributed directly to well-being. 'Social value' (Jordan 2007, 2008) was therefore an appropriate term for what was accumulated when such transactions were predominantly positive, and reduced when they were negative – stigmatising, imposed or coercive, as in compulsory 'workfare' or 'welfare-to-work' schemes (Jordan 2010a, b, 2019, 2020; Standing 2011, 2017).

It is important to recognise that the distinction between those interactions which enhance and those which diminish social value is not simple and absolute. An example will illustrate this. The prison and probation services in England evolved over centuries; prisons were chaotic local institutions until the 1830s, when they began to be re-organised, with new buildings constructed on the principles of Bentham's *Panopticon* (1791), allowing inmates in single cells to be regularly observed by staff. These institutions were managed by the Home Office, with the aim of isolating prisoners from each other, and the hope that – with guidance from a chaplain – they could reflect on their actions and emerge as reformed characters.

The probation service was gradually established as an adjunct to the magistrates' courts from the 1870s, and was pioneered by religiously motivated staff; it was formally recognised and became a national organisation in the first decade of the twentieth century. Both prison governors and probation officers were strongly influenced after the First World War by reformers (the prisons especially by Sir Alexander Paterson, who had introduced education and sport to open establishments, along the lines of the middle-class boarding school traditions). They were committed to the idea that offenders could respond to kindness and care, informed by new psychological influences as well as religious ones, and expressed in personal relationships.

The transformation achieved by this movement was most vividly captured by Brendan Behan in his *Borstal Boy* (1958), an account of how he, as a very young IRA activist who had attempted a terrorist attack, completely changed his view of English society and of human relationships more generally through his experiences of kindness, concern and counselling in a young offenders' institution. This led to him becoming a distinguished Irish literary figure.

The point here is that the English prison system was still coercive, in the sense that all inmates were held against their will. Furthermore, as I can attest from having worked for a year as a prison officer in the mid-1960s, and for ten years as a probation officer thereafter, these institutions still contained some staff whose motives were primarily ones of control and containment. But there were also some in prisons, and many in the probation service, who saw their relationships with offenders as opportunities for changing the orientation of those who had broken the law, and encouraging them into constructive use of their considerable energies in ways that enhanced economic and social value in their society.

Regrettably, the best of these traditions have been difficult to sustain in recent years, as both services have become dominated by managerialist ideas and systems and market-based organisational structures; the probation service has been re-organised several times as these proved to be unreliable and ineffective. But the earlier experiences are still evidence of the possibility of systems which embody both positive and negative social value, and can sustain a productive tension and balance between the two.

An Opportunity for Change

This historical example shows how an unpromising moment (in Behan's case, Britain's lowest hour during the Second World War, when the IRA was opportunistically sapping its morale, as its icons, Pearse and Connelly, had attempted to do during the First World War) could supply an opportunity to enhance social value. The dramatic fall in national income brought about by the coronavirus pandemic forces a re-assessment of priorities in social policies across the board, and especially in income maintenance.

One of the more improbable events of the global crisis was the decision by US president Donald Trump to grant $1200 to every US citizen earning less than $75,000 a year, with an additional $500 for each child. At a stroke, something akin to an unconditional Universal Basic Income (UBI), advocated for decades by some political philosophers (Van Parijs 1995; Offe 1992; Barry 1997), economists (Standing 2011, 2017; Parker 1989; Purdy 1995) and social theorists (Jordan 1973, 1996, 2006, 2010a), but implemented only in states with windfall mineral wealth (Alaska, Namibia and Mongolia), was being rolled out in the world's richest and most powerful country. Although the UK's response was far more fragmented and unconvincing, it too took some measures to supply more generalised income support, while the Spanish government unapologetically introduced an unconditional UBI.

Although this was primarily a response to the collapse in national incomes, these measures could also be seen as attempts to conserve social value, at a time when there was a risk of economic and social conflict, and a threat to morale and solidarity among citizens. The study of well-being largely assumed that Western liberal democracies enjoyed the highest rates of SWB because of the civil rights of individuals and the freedoms of a market economy. Dictatorships and states experiencing civil wars, as in some Middle Eastern countries, had lower levels of SWB, and also of trust between citizens (Helliwell 2003).

So the question is whether this can additionally be an opportunity to re-assess the direction which the most developed societies have taken in the past 50 years, not least in the structures of the service sectors of their economies. It seems clear that the stagnation in levels of SWB (and hence social value) reflected growing inequalities of income and wealth which arose through globalisation, with most workers in these services performing low-skilled and low-paid tasks, serving the needs of a rich minority – retailing, home improvements, child care, gardening and the public services. Income taxation, which reaches right down the earnings scale, overlapping with earnings subsidisation, is another factor (the 'Poverty Trap'). The state subsidises these low-paid, often part-time or occasional employments, and the benefits authorities force those facing such disincentives, and hence reluctant to do this work, into performing it. But after the coronavirus pandemic, must this pattern be recreated?

It should be possible to use this interruption, which may last many months or even years, to re-assess the direction we have taken for four decades or more, since the combination of globalisation and wage supplements became the orthodoxy of the late 1970s. Would it not be far better to create services for all, aimed at improving the well-being that has stagnated for as long as inequality has been growing and state coercion expanding in scope? What form might such services take – activities which would be more satisfying for workers, and more beneficial for all citizens, who could use them more equally? And according to which principles should income be distributed throughout the population?

The pandemic immediately evoked the use of state power to control and direct the isolation of households and the use of labour power, to an extent which was unique in peace time. It also saw the immediate adoption of large tax rises and new distribution systems. If such rapid changes were accepted by citizens without significant protest, why could they not be retained and extended?

The tragic consequences of the pandemic for thousands may supply a unique opportunity to address these questions, which have been evaded for decades, as much by social democratic as by conservative political parties. Just as we have turned a blind eye to the destruction of the earth's environment, we have allowed inequality of material resources and citizens' rights to grow to monstrous proportions. How did this come about?

Conclusions

There are several levels at which policy-makers and professionals (such as social and community workers) might intervene to try to increase social well-being, and hence social value. The largest-scale of these is that of whole societies and federations, such as the EU (Deeming 2013; Deeming and Hayes 2012; Deeming and Jones 2015). These would involve more robust and effective welfare systems (health services and income maintenance schemes) to address the factors which are known to reduce well-being, including inequality in status as well as material resources.

The second is to link these more reliably with the everyday lives of citizens. Several authors have argued that well-being studies represent a paradigm shift in the ways that policies can be understood to impact on lived experiences, and that these insights should guide new professional practices worldwide (Bache and Reardon 2016; Bache and Scott 2018; Thin 2012; Wren Lewis 2019; Wallace and Schmuekler 2012; White and Jha 2012).

This book will address the issues raised at both these levels. By focusing on social value – how it is created or destroyed in relationships at every level – it will clarify how both policy-makers and professional practitioners can more effectively increase well-being, and avoid reducing it.

The central point here is that well-being (SWB) is an *outcome* of relationships, experiences and conditions, as is its opposite, dissatisfaction, frustration and resentment. Social value is what is created or destroyed in the *processes* of these relationships, experiences and conditions. The UK government has started to adopt policies which address these processes, as will be shown in the next chapter.

References

Bache, I., & Reardon, L. (2016). *The Politics and Policy of Wellbeing: Understanding the Rise and Significance of a New Agenda.* Cheltenham: Edward Elgar.

Bache, I., & Scott, K. (Eds). (2018). *The Politics of Well-Being: Theory, Policy and Practice.* Basingstoke: Palgrave Macmillan.

Barry, B. (1997). The Attractions of Basic Income. In J. Franklin (Ed.), *Equality* (pp. 157–171). London: Institute for Public Policy Research.

Behan, B. (1958). *Borstal Boy.* Dublin: Arena Books.

Bentham, J. (1791). Panopticon, or the Inspection House. In J. Bowring (Ed.), *The Complete Works of Jeremy Bentham* (Vol. 4). Edinburgh: Tait (1843).

Deeming, C. (2013). Addressing the Social Determinants of Subjective Wellbeing: The Latest Challenge for Social Policy. *Journal of Social Policy, 42*(3), 541–565.

Deeming, C., & Hayes, D. (2012). Worlds of Welfare Capitalism and Wellbeing: A Multilevel Analysis. *Journal of Social Policy, 41*(4), 811–829.

Deeming, C., & Jones, K. (2015). Investigating the Macro-Determinants of Self-Related Health and Wellbeing Using the European Social Survey: Methodological Innovations across Countries and Time. *International Journal of Sociology, 45*(4), 256–285.

Haagh, L. (2019). *The Case for Universal Basic Income.* Cambridge: Polity.

Helliwell, J. F. (2003). How's Life? Combining Individual and National Variables to Explain Subjective Well-Being. *Economic Modelling, 20*, 331–360.

Jordan, B. (1973). *Paupers: The Making of the New Claiming Class.* London: Routledge and Kegan Paul.

Jordan, B. (1996). *A Theory of Poverty and Social Exclusion.* Cambridge: Polity.

Jordan, B. (2006). *Social Policy for the Twenty-First Century: New Perspectives, Big Issues.* Cambridge: Polity.

Jordan, B. (2007). *Social Work and Well-Being.* Lyme Regis: Russell House.

Jordan, B. (2008). *Welfare and Well-Being: Social Value in Public Policy.* Bristol: Policy Press.

Jordan, B. (2010a). *Why the Third Way Failed: Economics, Morality and Social Policy.* Bristol: Policy Press.

Jordan, B. (2010b). *What's Wrong with Social Policy and How to Fix It.* Cambridge: Polity.

Jordan, B. (2019). *Authoritarianism and How to Counter It*. Basingstoke: Palgrave Macmillan.

Jordan, B. (2020). *Automation and Human Solidarity*. Basingstoke: Palgrave Macmillan.

Kahneman, D. (1999). Objective Well-Being. In D. Kahneman, E. Diener, & N. Schwartz (Eds.), *Well-Being: Foundations of Hedonic Psychology*. New York: Russell Sage Foundation.

Layard, R. (2005). *Happiness: Lessons from a New Science*. London: Allen Lane.

Offe, C. (1992). A Non-Productivist Design for Social Policies. In P. Van Parijs (Ed.), *Arguing for Basic Income: Ethical Foundations for a Radical Reform*. London: Routledge.

Parker, H. (1989). *Instead of the Dole: An Enquiry into Integration of the Tax and Benefit System*. London: Routledge.

Purdy, D. (1995). Citizenship, Basic Income and the State. *New Left Review, 208*, 427–439.

Standing, G. (2011). *The Precariat: The New Dangerous Class*. London: Bloomsbury.

Standing, G. (2017). *The Corruption of Capitalism: Why* Rentiers *Thrive and Work Does Not Pay*. London: Biteback.

Thin, N. (2012). *Social Happiness: Theory into Policy and Practice*. Bristol: Policy Press.

Van Parijs, P. (1995). *Real Freedom for All: What (If Anything) Can Justify Capitalism?* Oxford: Clarendon Press.

Wallace, J., & Schmuekler, K. (2012). *Shifting the Dial: From Well-Being Measurement to Policy Practice*. Dunfermline: Carnegie Trust/Institute for Public Policy Research.

White, S., & Jha, S. (2012). Towards an Interdisciplinary Approach to Well-Being: Life Histories and Self-Determining Theory in Rural Zambia. *Social Science and Medicine, 212*, 153–166.

Wilkinson, R., & Pickett, K. (2009). *The Spirit Level: Why More Equal Societies (Almost Always) Do Better*. London: Allen Lane.

Wren Lewis, S. (2019). *The Happiness Problem: Expecting Better in an Uncertain World*. Bristol: Policy Press.

CHAPTER 2

The Genesis of the Social Value Problem

Abstract Although the concept of social value is new to social policy (Jordan, *Welfare and Well-Being: Social Value in Public Policy*. Bristol: Policy Press, 2008), the problem of its reliable maintenance in economic and political relations has been present for the UK for at least five decades. The division in the working class through subsidisation of low wages meant that the interests of taxpayers and claimants of such support were antagonistic, and this undermined the capacity of governments to sustain policies for the common good (Jordan, *The Common Good: Citizenship, Morality and Self-Interest*. Oxford: Blackwell, 1986). Yet the concept of social value did enter the field of social policy through its adoption in legislation in 2011, and very widely by voluntary organisations thereafter, and finally by the NHS in the past few years.

Keywords Social division • Voluntary sector • Common good • Health service

In retrospect, the key moment in the UK was the early 1970s. A Conservative government was still trying to sustain the One Nation policies of the Macmillan era, without yet having recognised the full implications of the decline of the manufacturing industry, or the phenomenon we now call globalisation. The trades union movement was divided, but the militant wing, led by Arthur Scargill's mineworkers, recognised an

B. Jordan, *Social Value in Public Policy*,
https://doi.org/10.1007/978-3-030-60421-9_2

opportunity to hold the government to ransom. It was then still plausible for militants to push for a Cuban-style revolution, which would overthrow capitalism, and substitute a regime in which the state commanded and directed productive forces. The miners' strike of 1974 caused the Heath government to call an election and resign.

This crisis marked the start of a process by which the UK's relative decline in the global economy was accompanied by a fall in the share of national income going to labour (which has continued ever since), and a corresponding rise in that going to capital, most prominently (except during the banking crisis of 2008–9) to finance capital. Part of the explanation for this is that the kinds of services in which workers have been increasingly employed have not been susceptible to improvements in productivity (Gershuny 1983) – even those associated with the digital revolution and Artificial Intelligence (AI). But living standards have benefited from the ever-growing productivity of manufacturing and processing in Asia, South America and most recently Africa, making imported goods (including food and clothes) cheaper for consumers in the West.

So the beneficiaries of the great shift foreseen by Karl Marx in *Capital* (1877, pp. 414–80 and 712–4) were not only bankers and financial traders, but also the lawyers, doctors and university researchers who served the needs of capitalism, and the public services which both employed and controlled a high proportion of the working class. This book will analyse how the decisions made 40 years ago have increasingly shaped the policies adopted ever since (and their outcomes) and how the present crisis might supply the opportunity for a radical change in direction.

There is really nothing new about this turn of events, the possibility of which was recognised by David Ricardo (1817) at the onset of the Industrial Revolution in the UK, 60 years before Marx's account. In Chapter 31 of his *Principles of Political Economy and Taxation*, Ricardo recognised that the *substitution* of new machines for human labour, without corresponding increases in output, would cause redundancy (pp. 264–7), but he thought that this was unlikely to occur for more than short periods, within a long-term tendency towards economic growth. Marx argued that it would signal the final stage of capitalist development, and contended that, without a revolution, it would result in a perpetual growth in the class of 'paupers' (1877, pp. 712–3). If we use the definition of that class as being those who by virtue of their dependence on state subsidies of their earnings are subject to coercion by the authorities, then this is precisely the term appropriate for a class whose numbers have been increasing ever since the early 1970s in the UK (Jordan 1973).

Is this class condemned to expand perpetually over time, in a way foreshadowed by the mass lay-offs associated with the coronavirus pandemic? It certainly did so in the UK up to 2011, when its peak (some 70 per cent of those members of the workforce living in households with children) was abruptly cut back by David Cameron's intervention to devalue Universal Credit payments. But the enormous rise during the coronavirus pandemic (a million new claims for UC during the final two weeks of March, 2020) may well point to a structural change in the labour market, as a whole range of services arising from the wealth of the top 10 per cent of the population, and the coercion of the bottom 30–50 per cent receiving UC, becomes institutionalised during a long, slow recovery.

This helps explain another phenomenon associated with the pandemic – the sudden increase in publications and debates about the proposal for an unconditional Universal Basic Income (UBI). Not only *The Guardian*, but also *The Times*, *The Daily Telegraph* (Sam Benstead, 19th March), *The Financial Times* (Daniel Susskind, 20th March), *The Independent* (Jon Stone, 27th April) and even the *Daily Mail on-line* and *The Sun* (Alexander Brown, 22nd April) have published articles specifically advocating UBI or some version of a payment for all but a few citizens. As 'Pause the System' demonstrators held a mass protest outside Parliament explicitly calling for UBI (Channel 4 TV, *News*, 16th March), Frances O'Grady, General Secretary of the TUC, hinted at 'added payments' during the lay-off, and Dame Louise Casey, former government adviser, said all benefits should be supplemented (ibid.).

Inequality of earnings was not explicitly linked with the discovery that rates of well-being had been stagnating for so many decades, but it seemed certain to be part of the explanation of this phenomenon in the UK and USA. Although economic growth had been slow and fitful, it had occurred, and some citizens had grown very rich, while others – the educated middle classes – had consolidated their security for generations by virtue of the soaring value of their family homes. The contrast with poor members of communities, and especially those in social housing, was a stark one (Jordan et al. 1992, 1994).

A New Direction in Policy

So it seemed that, while the intimate relationships of families were the most important components of SWB, and those of association and community were significant factors, the civic relations between citizens were also relevant for differences between local, regional and national averages. Just as economic relationships produced income and wealth, so these relationships yielded 'social value' (Jordan 2007, 2008). This concept quickly entered the official vocabulary, with reference to the contribution of specific policies to the well-being of communities. In the Public Services (Social Value) Act of 2012, the Coalition government put through a short piece of legislation requiring all public authorities, in contracting for any commodity or service, to 'consider how what is proposed to be procured might improve the economic, social and environmental well-being of the relevant area' (sec.1.3(a)).

At the same time, a new organisation, Social Value UK, took the lead in promoting social value in the voluntary sector, in line with the Act. It seeks to identify and enhance the benefits received by individuals from collective bodies, hitherto often unrecognised by those bodies themselves. The National Health Service (NHS) was one of the last public bodies to join up, and in 2020 the construction industry was admitted as a member, having recognised and acknowledged its notoriety over issues of flood prevention, conservation and sustainability, and seeing this as a public-relations opportunity. A national Social Value conference, hosted by Social Value UK and the Social Value Portal, was held, with 700 delegates, only a handful of whom were from the NHS, but including some from schools and universities.

This represented a rapid growth in the use of social value as a criterion for decisions in both the public and the voluntary sectors in the UK, yet it still lacked a clear definition. For example, the Social Value Portal's website states that it is 'a social enterprise on a mission to promote business and community well-being', and gives as its second priority 'to support regional businesses', as well as quantifying the return to communities of each pound spent under its auspices; this suggests commercial rather than face-to-face relationships.

It seems as if something present in human interactions ever since the very first emergence of groups and tribes has suddenly been identified, given a name and then commercialised through market processes. It looks like an extraordinarily accelerated process akin to the one identified by

Adam Smith (1759), by which what had been informal trading among individuals and groups over centuries was institutionalised in regional, national and international markets, without the conscious intentions of governments – by the operation of a providential 'invisible hand'. But what is usually forgotten is that Smith's book was called *The Theory of Moral Sentiments*, and its main content was about how – through 'sympathy' or 'fellow-feeling' – people came to live together and co-operate at all.

The idea of 'social value' simply draws attention to what is being produced or depleted in all these relationships, in the form of the various elements that constitute SWB, and hence are quite distinct from what is measured by money, and capable of being bought and sold. Some of these elements may be derived from or enhanced by the 'consumption' of goods and experiences (as in a good meal after an enjoyable evening at a cinema), but they are aspects of human societies, in all the complexities of their bonds and divisions, and not of economies, which are susceptible to objective (rather than subjective, self-assessed) quantification.

The attempt to quantify and commercialise social value is certainly contrary to Smith's advocacy of a society sustained by 'moral sentiments' and 'sympathy', as much as by 'the pedlar principle of turning every penny' (1776, bk III, ch. iv, para 17). When the Public Sector Executive, in its 'episode 005 of the #WeArePSE Podcast' (27 January, 2020), claimed that 'understanding the economic benefits of social value, embedding social value in how businesses deliver' is 'transforming the relationship between the public and the private sector' through its impact on communities, Smith might have felt that this balance had been upset in a potentially damaging way.

Conclusions

Turning points in history involve the substitution of one set of criteria for major decisions by another, and the adoption of new institutions to reflect this change. Pestilence has been the spark for such turning points in the past, most notably when the Black Death wiped out more than half the population of England in 1348–50, leading to the process by which the leaders of a much-reduced peasantry, Watt Tyler and John Ball, confronted the king at the head of a mass protest in 1381, and won freedom from feudal duties and tithes. Increasingly in the centuries which followed, rights and liberties were at stake in political contests and civil conflicts, with liberal democracy as the eventual outcome.

Nothing as dramatic as this is yet associated with the coronavirus pandemic, and the death rates are mercifully small by comparison. But the crisis came when authoritarianism was on the rise throughout the world, rather as it had been in the 1930s. It might re-enforce this tendency, as it seems to be doing in China (and especially in Hong Kong) where the Communist Party leadership has taken the opportunities it affords to clamp down on dissidents and impose draconian controls. But elsewhere there does seem to be evidence of a recognition that the end of lockdown, during which the power of the state was used to supply services and redistribute income in more radical ways than for many decades, could allow the opportunity for a change in direction.

For a start, although many firms and larger industries showed remarkable flexibility in switching their production of anything from whisky to vacuum cleaners and fashion accessories to supplies of hand-sanitiser, respirators and face masks, this was (for the most part) an example of public-spiritedness and solidarity, not the efficient functioning of markets. Just as there were millions of volunteers to help isolated elderly and disabled people, there were also examples of opportunists buying up toilet paper and plastic gowns in bulk, and selling them at inflated prices on the internet. Markets were equally good at serving the greed of profiteers as signalling the need for various forms of protective equipment.

There is no evidence from the research on SWB over the past 40 years that markets – in whose service the public sectors of Western capitalist democracies had been privatised to a considerable extent – contributed to the well-being of citizens through this expansion in their influence within those economies; if anything, the evidence points to an association with growing inequalities, and reductions in the social value accumulated in relationships, except among the richer and better-educated classes. There were no clear exceptions to this tendency among Western liberal democracies.

So it would take a major political push to bring about the kinds of changes conducive to gains in social value in the recovery from the pandemic. But it would be a mistake to claim that any such movement or ideological shift can take the form of a coherent and consistent set of ideas and practices. The great transformations in history have seen a somewhat chaotic mixture of theories and proposals, with many inconsistencies and contradictions.

Furthermore, this chaos is emerging as part of the science of cognition and perception in recent research studies, and from projects developing AI.

The human brain has 86 billion nerve cells; AI has long been predicted to exceed its capacities for intelligent thought (Walmsley and de Sousa 2010). But – as in physics, where quantum mechanics has still to be reconciled with general relativity – neuroscience has yet to be integrated with unconscious mental process research, electrophysiology, pharmacology, optico-genetics, gene-editing and abstract modelling – tasks for which the long-running 'Human Brain Project' has so far proved inadequate. A breakthrough is still awaited (Cobb 2020).

In social policy, the equivalent of this has been the constant failure of rationally designed measures, aimed to use market processes to function across the service sector, and to allow citizens choice over collective provision; they have foundered on the determined resistance of those excluded (by virtue of poverty, disability or ill health) from benefiting through such processes. The obvious example of this was Margaret Thatcher's reforms of the public services, which proved so costly (in terms of rising crime, family breakdown, benefits fraud, alcoholism and substance abuse) that they made the costs of policing, prisons and insurance premiums unacceptable to the electorate (Jordan et al. 1992, 1994; Jordan 1987, 1996).

All this implies that the breakthrough to more radical change is more likely to come through a fortuitous combination of apparently inconsistent and unconnected contingencies than a grand master-plan. This book will explore some of the possible elements that might combine to create the circumstances for such a transformation.

References

Benstead, S. (2020, March 19). Universal Basic Income: What Is It, How Does It Work and Could It Help Fight the Economic Crisis?: Distributing Cash Directly to All Citizens Could Lift the Economic Burden of the Shutdown. *Daily Telegraph*.

Brown, A. (2020, April 22). Britain Can Move Towards a Universal Basic Income – Just Look at Spain. *The Sun*.

Cobb, M. (2020). *The Idea of the Brain: A History*. London: Profile Books.

Gershuny, J. I. (1983). *Social Innovation and the Division of Labour*. Oxford: Oxford University Press.

Jordan, B. (1973). *Paupers: The Making of the New Claiming Class*. London: Routledge and Kegan Paul (Republished, 2019).

Jordan, B. (1986). *The Common Good: Citizenship, Morality and Self-Interest*. Oxford: Blackwell.

Jordan, B. (1987). *Rethinking Welfare*. Oxford: Blackwell.

Jordan, B. (1996). *A Theory of Poverty and Social Exclusion*. Cambridge: Polity.
Jordan, B. (2007). *Social Work and Well-Being*. Lyme Regis: Russell House Press.
Jordan, B. (2008). *Welfare and Well-Being: Social Value in Public Policy*. Bristol: Policy Press.
Jordan, B., James, S., Kay, H., & Redley, M. (1992). *Trapped in Poverty? Labour Market Decisions in Low-Income Households*. London: Routledge.
Jordan, B., Redley, M., & James, S. (1994). *Putting the Family First: Identities, Decisions, Citizenship*. London: UCL Press.
Marx, K. (1877). *Capital: A Critique of Political Economy*. London: Penguin (1977).
Ricardo, D. (1817). *Principles of Political Economy and Taxation*. Edinburgh: Dent (1912).
Smith, A. (1759). *The Theory of Moral Sentiments* (pp. 7–280). New York: Harper and Row (1948).
Smith, A. (1776). *An Inquiry Concerning the Nature and Causes of the Wealth of Nations*. Oxford: Clarendon Press (1976).
Stone, J. (2020, April 27). Public Support Universal Basic Income, Job Guarantee and Rent Controls to Respond to Coronavirus Pandemic, Poll Finds. *The Independent*.
Walmsley, A., & de Sousa, E. (2010). *Philosophies of Science*. Paper Presented at an International Summer School, 'Theory and Philosophy', Blackwater Castle, Cork, 3rd May.

CHAPTER 3

How Social Value Works

Abstract The coronavirus pandemic forced governments to temporarily sacrifice economic prosperity for the health and well-being of their citizens. The lock-down had all the more impact in developed countries because so much economic activity has come to take the form of face-to-face services. People responded by being far more cautious about their interactions with others; they self-enforced a new set of rules, which in turn have shaped each other's behaviour, very quickly becoming a new norm (David Halpern, Head of the 'Nudge Unit' for Behavioural Psychology, on BBC Radio 4, 'Start the Week', 27 April, 2020).

Keywords Pandemic • Lock-down • Literature • Psychoanalysis

The lock-down during the pandemic was a rare example of well-being trumping economic gain in the everyday process of public life. Even where family and community interactions have resisted market penetration, it is rare for political leaderships to give priority to social value. The only clear exception to this rule is the Kingdom of Bhutan in the Himalayas; there, the official goal of government is to maximise 'Gross National *Happiness*' (a synonym for 'well-being' in Layard 2005) rather than Gross National Product (GNP). Even if this is largely a rationalisation for preserving an

B. Jordan, *Social Value in Public Policy*,
https://doi.org/10.1007/978-3-030-60421-9_3

archaic hierarchy, based on early Buddhist tradition, it is still an interesting principle, which might be a precedent for other societies.

Although the recent conversion of service organisations in the UK to the idea of social value has been sudden and perhaps quite woolly and unconvincing, it does signify a recognition that conventional economic analysis has failed to capture the most significant features of the transformation of advanced societies. If economic growth becomes less feasible and desirable in the face of global warming and the sustainability crisis, then humanity needs some dimension on which to progress, if life is not to become no more than a struggle against losing ground.

The qualitative evaluations which were pioneered by the well-being researchers now invite exploration of the processes of social interaction through which gains and losses in SWB occur. Not only social psychology (the discipline which originally gave us ways to measure well-being) but also education, mental health and social work all use relationships as the medium for their professional tasks, and can therefore be seen as dealing in social value (Jordan 2007, 2008).

In this chapter, I shall explore how these processes were understood before the advent of SWB research made this whole topic a focus for public policy. It would not be a gross oversimplification to say that emotions and relationships were seldom seen as subjects for the scientific studies which conferred status and commanded large research funding. Psychiatry as a branch of medicine was rather low on the ladder of prestige, and many mental hospital facilities were archaic, isolated and redolent with stigma for their inmates (Goffman 1967), and to some extent for their staff also.

Although these features were reduced to some extent by the movement of long-term patients into smaller units, and the greater availability of outpatient treatments of many kinds, as well as a variety of therapists in private practice, much of this stigma persists. One irony of the history of psychiatry has been that Sigmund Freud's theories and insights, by far the best known outside the specialist medical field, have given rise to a limited number of therapists trained in this tradition, but have enormously influenced the arts – literature, the theatre and even the visual arts – over the past 100 or so years.

I shall argue that ideas of well-being and social value permeate these arts, and most explicitly literature, where the processes through which relationships either enhance or undermine the flourishing of the characters can be so vividly and profoundly explored and illustrated. The relevance of literary studies for the analysis of SWB and social value has hitherto been a neglected opportunity.

Research on SWB by economists deals in comparisons between categories such as occupations, incomes, age groups, neighbourhoods and educational attainments, but practitioners such as doctors, teachers and social workers need to be able to understand – and, if possible, intervene in – the processes by which some people accumulate social value, and others waste or squander it. This book is intended to inform, and perhaps improve, their practice.

The novel as a literary form flourished in the nineteenth century, as a way of exploring how human relationships created an arena for the development of personalities, either fulfilling their potentials or squandering them, and allowing a few of those who seemed to be heading down the latter path to be redeemed by love or friendship, while some of the former were destroyed in such processes. Whereas the economic research gives few clues about *how* some societies foster and promote relationships that increase well-being while others do not, these microcosms of their societies do, at their best, enable their readers to make connections between the personal and the political levels – the supreme example perhaps being Leo Tolstoy's *War and Peace* (1874–6).

Novels are much better at demonstrating the complexity and fragility of human relationships than they are at showing how policies might allow them to flourish. However, the challenge to governments posed by SWB statistics is made much clearer by these insights; there is no room for unsubstantiated optimism in any attempt to influence social value through public policy.

Above all, relationships are embedded in an all-embracing context of power which, even when it is obvious in retrospect, at the time is veiled and obscured by ideology and rhetoric. Mutual aid and sympathy, as well as romantic love and intimacy, are parts of the natural order; yet they are often marginalised and devalued by their political context.

Intimate and Civic Relationships

In the nineteenth century, both British and French novels, and later Russian ones, transcended the scope of their antecedents in the previous one – such as Samuel Richardson's *Pamela* (1740) and Henry Fielding's *Tom Jones* (1749), in which usually naïve young country people's adventures among knowing and corrupt city dwellers supplied comedy before their eventual successful transition into the urban scene – by illustrating the complexities of romantic and civic relationships as the class system evolved in conditions of gradual urbanisation and industrialisation.

Although Jane Austen's heroines are mostly based, as she herself was, in rural districts, their suitors are often city-dwellers in the professions or armed services, and the plots of the novels centre around relationships which are as much educational (of the emotions and the morals, under conditions of inequality, separation and various forms of adversity) as they are romantic. The overall impetus of their narratives tends towards an improvement in social relations between the classes and the sexes, in which women and the church play leading roles, albeit usually low-key and modest ones.

This is often achieved through claims of social value by middle-class women or impoverished families in relation to wealthy and well-born characters. Social value is derived from their capacities to sustain witty and agile interactions as well as intimate and affectionate ones.

In Austen's *Pride and Prejudice* (1813), the central characters reflect the emerging tensions in relationships between the landed aristocracy and the growing educated middle class. Fitzwilliam Darcy is explicitly self-critical and conflicted over his overwhelming attraction to Elizabeth Bennet, a young woman from a family with little property; she herself is in denial about hers to him, because she interprets all his behaviour as reflecting a sense of social superiority. It is only when each can value the other as a person, unencumbered by these class-biased perceptions, that their mutual love can flourish.

A more extreme example of the political context for social value is *Mansfield Park* (1814), in which the tact and humility of the central character, the humbly born Fanny Price, and her socially responsible (eventual) clergyman husband, Edmund Bertram, is contrasted with the self-indulgent and extravagant behaviour of her rich cousins and their friends, into whose household she moves as an exploited care assistant. Here there is no ambiguity about the ways in which wealth and privilege can distort the potential social value of relationships.

In the world of Charles Dickens' novels, a much wider range of rural and urban characters, from the rootless street-urchins of *Oliver Twist* (1837–8) to the emotionally frozen aristocrats Lord and Lady Dedlock in *Bleak House* (1852–3), inhabit a complex society in the process of rapid economic transformation. Here again, the heroine of the latter, Esther Summerson, conducts herself with exemplary virtue through the labyrinth of suffering, folly and poverty that she encounters, eventually finding a loving relationship with the virtuous doctor Allan Woodcourt. She is a kind of model of the social workers who emerged from the cities' middle classes in the final quarter of the century (Jordan 1976, ch. 6).

It was a mark of the more pessimistic climate of the later years of that century that few such characters are to be found in the defining novels of that age. For instance, in Thomas Hardy's *Jude the Obscure* (1894), the eponymous orphan sets out on a search for self-improvement through education, only to contract an impulsive marriage to the earthier Arabella, then leave her and start a relationship with his cousin, Sue. The nightmare death of their children is the prelude to his reunion with Arabella, as Jude abandons his early ideals. Hardy used these relationships to explore the passing of an age of unreflective peasant matrimony, often drunken and careless, to one in which every thought and action is ambiguous and fraught. In his preface to the 1912 edition of the novel, Hardy questioned the whole moral basis for the institution of marriage, and argued for the availability of instant divorce.

In art, too, the social value of obscure peasants and their environments was celebrated in Gauguin and Van Gogh's paintings in Brittany and Flanders, and then of 'primitive' Polynesians in Tahiti. They are portrayed as having natural qualities and customs which are of at least equal value to those of the Western bourgeoisie.

These ambiguities and ambivalences became even more marked in the literature of the twentieth century. In D.H. Lawrence's *Sons and Lovers* (1914), Paul is constantly unable to shake off the sense of a struggle between the flesh and the spirit; unlike his uncomplicated miner father, he was acutely aware of the risks of hurting a woman. Men like him 'preferred to suffer the miseries of celibacy, rather than risk the other person' (p. 341).

So, on the cusp of the transformation in economies and societies that was to take place during and immediately after the First World War, English literature reflected a shift in consciousness within relationships of intimacy, both denying them the easy pleasures of the eighteenth-century romps, and anticipating the much more stormy and violent expression of these conflicts in the twentieth century.

These were often more preoccupied with issues of totalitarian politics (in the lead-up to the Second World War), as in George Orwell, and the complexities of identity and class, as in the post-war novels *Saturday Night and Sunday Morning*, Alan Sillitoe, 1958, and *A Kestrel for a Knave*, Barry Hines, 1968, which were both made into memorable films. But the enduring contribution of the earlier traditions of the literary form had meanwhile influenced the intellectual development of the whole century.

Society and Psychology

If we are to understand how social value is created, distributed and destroyed, it is vital to base this on a reliable analysis of the complexities of relationships. In the period after the mid-nineteenth century, the novel supplied an ideal vehicle for this process; it would have been just as valid to illustrate this in those of Flaubert and Zola, or Dostoyevsky and Tolstoy, as in their English contemporaries.

But it was in Austria and Germany that these complexities were analysed and theorised in the most sophisticated, academic way. Sigmund Freud became the leading figure in a movement which aimed to produce a scientific theory of the workings of the mind and of emotional experiences, and he carried this analysis over into a grand narrative about the history of social institutions as systems of social control. In *Civilization and Its Discontents* (1929), he set out to develop an account of how this sophisticated construction was 'built up on *renunciations* of instinctual gratifications....(T)he existence of civilisation presupposes the non-gratification (suppression, repression or something else?) of powerful instinctual urgencies' (pp. 43–8).

This account used metaphors from anthropology and history to explain these processes: 'Culture behaves towards sexuality...like a tribe or section of a population which has gained the upper hand and is exploiting the rest to its own advantage. Fear of revolt among the rest then becomes a motive for even stricter regulations. A high-water mark in this type of development has been reached in our Western European civilisation...(which) obtains a mastery over dangerous love of aggression in individuals by enfeebling and disarming it and setting up an institution within their minds to keep watch over it like a garrison in a conquered city' (pp. 48, 57).

There is a bitter irony, of course, in the fact that Freud wrote this only a few years before the rise of the Nazi dictatorship in Germany and Austria, from which he fled to England. Far from the inhibition of primitive instincts and drives, this was in many ways their brutal expression, and the Second World War and the Holocaust carried these to their most apocalyptic extremes. It was not inhibition which turned out to be the enemy, but the lack of it.

Conclusions

Nineteenth-century literature had illustrated how relationships were hazardous; people risked humiliation or destruction for the sake of love and fulfilment. But the politics of race reverted to the tribal competition between groups which characterised our early history, and on a massive scale, with deadly weapons. It was the nation which needed to be civilised as much as – or more than – the individual.

In the years after that war, the concept of welfare – as in the welfare state as a set of rights for citizens of a nation – largely displaced the notion that personal relationships characterised the culture or civilisation of a society. It was the expression of the democratic system which had defeated the totalitarianism of the Nazis, and stood against that of Stalinism, and it was individual freedom which was generalised outwards into the liberal, pluralistic polity.

If well-being was mentioned at all, it was expressed in the hybrid idea of 'health-and-well-being', in which the dominant element was the health services which, in the UK and in Europe, were developed as a massive improvement to the length, as well as the quality, of the lives of citizens. Well-being did not become a key concept for public services for another 40 or more years.

But in recent years, power-holders have once again become much more capable of masking their capacities to distort the distribution of social value, through both economic and political processes. When the coronavirus pandemic struck, governments which had been for years implementing austerity, public spending cuts and the coercion of poor people suddenly found the means to spend on benefits for all, health and social care.

So the question is what will happen once the crisis is over. Will the ways in which people have been revalued during the pandemic – nurses, care assistants, shop-workers and public transport employees, for example – and in which the general public have revealed themselves as neighbourly, helpful and demonstrating empathy and mutuality disappear and will things revert to their previous order?

In a wide-ranging discussion on YouTube ('The Flip', Spanner Films, 24 May, 2020), Caroline Lucas (Green Party MP), George Monbiot (writer on environmental issues) and Faisa Shaheen (trades unionist) discussed how the positive aspects of the crisis could be retained in its aftermath. Instead of allowing a tiny minority of the super-rich and political oligarchs ('psychopaths', as Monbiot called them) to control societies, the chance was there for myths to be dispelled, a Universal Basic Income scheme adopted, the real threat of climate change tackled, and social solidarities reconstructed.

The nature and consequences of social value-laden transactions, between individuals, classes and communities, have been at the heart of the literature, art and history of war and peace in the past three centuries. This book will explore whether the explicit theorising and empirical analysis of all of these in terms of this concept can influence future policy and politics.

References

Austen, J. (1813). *Pride and Prejudice.* London: Penguin Books (1965).

Austen, J. (1814). *Mansfield Park.* London: Penguin Books (1966).

Dickens, C. (1837–8). *Oliver Twist.* London: Chapman and Hall (1911).

Dickens, C. (1852–3). *Bleak House.* London: Chapman and Hall (1911).

Fielding, H. (1749). *Tom Jones, a Foundling.* London: Penguin Classics (1980).

Freud, S. (1929). Civilisation and Its Discontents. In *Civilisation, War and Death: Psycho-analytical Epitomes*, No. 4. London: Hogarth Press (1939).

Goffman, E. (1967). On Face Work: An Analysis of the Ritual Elements in Interaction. In *Interaction Ritual: Essays in Face-to-Face Behaviour* (pp. 1–46). New York: Doubleday Anchor.

Hardy, T. (1894). *Jude the Obscure.* London: Macmillan.

Hines, B. (1968). *A Kestrel for a Knave.* London: Penguin.

Jordan, B. (1976). *Freedom and the Welfare State.* Abingdon: Routledge and Kegan Paul (Republished, 2019).

Jordan, B. (2007). Social Value in Services for Children. *Journal of Children's Services, 5*, 53–70.

Jordan, B. (2008). *Welfare and Well-Being; Social Value in Public Policy.* Bristol: Policy Press.

Lawrence, D. H. (1914). *Sons and Lovers.* London: Penguin (1974).

Layard, R. (2005). *Happiness: Lessons from a New Science.* London: Allen Lane.

Richardson, S. (1740). *Pamela, or Virtue Rewarded.* London: Penguin Classics (1981).

Sillitoe, A. (1958). *Saturday Night and Sunday Morning.* London: W.H. Allen Ltd.

Tolstoy, L. (1874–6). *War and Peace.* London: Penguin Classics (1979).

CHAPTER 4

Social Control and Social Value

Abstract There is something about research and theory on well-being and social value that seems naïve. It appears to ignore the vast evidence of human suffering through the centuries, and right up to the present, from the mechanisms through which power-holders exercise social control. It is as if Subjective Well-being measures the extent to which idiotic humans can ignore the impact of these cruel and degrading systems on their lives.

Keywords Coercion • Power • Surveillance • Deviance

Social theory and social policy analysis has not lacked abundant evidence of the power dimension of social experience. Especially since the early 1970s, there has been a vast literature about social control, both analysing its processes and cataloguing its consequences. Furthermore, there is also a convincing case to be made for the idea that it is becoming more pervasive in its reach, and more sophisticated in the technological means for its exercise.

For instance, in her account of the growth in the penetration of everyday life of these technologies, Shoshana Zuboff (2019) describes how every aspect of present-day activities is monitored through the machinery of *Surveillance Capitalism*. Devices in the home such as thermostats, and everyday items like street cameras, mobile phones and credit cards, all

B. Jordan, *Social Value in Public Policy*,
https://doi.org/10.1007/978-3-030-60421-9_4

supply raw materials for 'prediction' products to be traded in 'behavioural futures markets'. These allow large corporations to nudge and steer us in a form of behaviour modification, predicting and controlling through secretly gathered data.

This is a new variant of the kind of analysis first advanced by the French historian and sociologist Michel Foucault in the 1970s. Recalling the model of social control invented by Jeremy Bentham at the dawn of the Industrial Revolution, he called this 'Panopticonism' – a form of totalitarian regulation and coercion through constant observation, originally deployed in prisons and Poor Law workhouses, as well as the earliest factories, in which external controls were eventually internalised by inmates. But under the latest regimes, subjects do not know that they are being watched (Thomas McMullan, 'What Does the Panopticon Mean in the Age of Digital Surveillance?' *The Guardian*, 23 July, 2020).

During the coronavirus pandemic, the Australian government introduced a phone app called COVIDSafe, used for contact tracing. It allowed the authorities to impose fines for breaches of its lock-down legislation; these were scheduled to continue for up to a year (Michael Bartos, *National Affairs*, 27 April, 2020).

The purpose of the latest systems of social control is as much to steer behaviour towards conformity with market-orientated norms (consumerism, embracing latest fashions and fads) as to reduce forms of deviance and illegality. This raises questions about whether statistics on SWB really measure 'happiness' of the kind created in positive relationships of all kinds, or whether they reflect adaptions to the various institutions by which regimes reward or punish behaviour in the systems of regulation in societies.

Theories of Deviance and Control

Perhaps one reason why theories about social control were so prevalent in the 1970s was that Western societies were emerging from the relative political consensus that followed the Second World War. The new ideas reflected the scepticism of a young generation, which had received a broader education than its parents', and was disillusioned with the social order their elders had come to accept. The new generation recognised and resented limits on the freedoms and aspirations of its members, and aspired to more creative possibilities than were available, especially in the industrial regions of the Western economies.

The philosopher who encapsulated the new aspirations was Herbert Marcuse, whose *Essay on Liberation* was published in 1969. He argued that corporate capitalism exercised insidious controls which imperceptibly conditioned populations to the requirements of technological production and consumption (p. 11). This had created 'a second nature of man which ties him libidinally and aggressively to the commodity form' and which 'militates against any change that would disrupt or perhaps abolish this dependence of man on a market ever more filled with merchandise' (ibid.).

This in turn created 'a social system [which] reproduces, by indoctrination and integration, a self-perpetuating conservative majority' (p. 69). A revolutionary 'New Man' would emerge from youth culture, with a different culture, language and impulses, and 'an instinctual barrier against cruelty, brutality and ugliness' (p. 21); the process of liberation would bring a socialist Utopia, and a transformation of all social relationships. It was such visionary writings which inspired the new generation.

The interactionist school of sociologists, led by Howard Becker (1974), had also studied subterranean and subversive cultures, such as that of drug-users, and how they defied the agencies for social control (Young 1971). They drew attention to the ways in which state interventions which labelled such behaviour as deviant tended to increase the alienation and disaffection of the groups in question. These ideas tended to glorify the rebellious groups as standard-bearers of a new age of liberation, which would prevail against systems of social control and usher in new freedoms for all.

But such notions receded as the market-minded regimes of Margaret Thatcher and Ronald Reagan came to power. Their programmes for privatisation of public services dampened the libertarians' disdain for state control; it was minorities of those who lived in marginal districts and relied on benefits for their livelihoods who were worst hit. Their 'deviance' was a response to poverty and exclusion, not bourgeois alienation (Jordan et al. 1992; Jordan 1996).

Within a decade, the 'choice' and 'liberty' that had become the watchwords of the UK and US regimes had penetrated to the former Soviet Bloc countries' citizens (US security services were said to have subverted their regimes by broadcasting endless pictures of supermarket shelves in the West). Such disciplines as were exercised by their new rulers seemed quite generous after the controls they had endured for more than 40 years.

So it has only been since the financial crisis of 2008–9 and the austerity years which followed that explicit issues of social control have again arisen for a new generation on both sides of the former Iron Curtain. Indeed, in all the developed countries, the prospects of young people had been severely limited by the absence of any growth in real earnings for more than 30 years; hence the mass protest marches (some, as in France, by middle-aged as well as young citizens) of the most recent decade, as those who feel dispossessed signal their disillusion with the prospect of a decline in their standards of living, compared with those of previous generations.

Many protests have been met by quite violent counter-measures by the police. This has been particularly the case in France, where the *Gilets Jaunes* have mobilised weekly over many months, and challenged the authorities in several regions and cities. Disappointment with the Macron presidency has led to increasing disillusion about France's future, and a long-term issue about social control in a political culture with a revolutionary history, and where theories of social control had been extensively developed since the 1970s (Foucault 1975).

Conclusions

The coronavirus pandemic brought about an economic recession far deeper than that associated with the financial crisis of 2008–9. The fact that this was the result of policies aimed at saving lives by reducing person-to-person contacts meant that it commanded very general popular support, but the consequences for incomes – declines of up to a third among those laid off – led some economists to question whether these measures might even cause more deaths (through deprivation) than they saved through social isolation.

In a BBC Radio 4 programme titled 'Will the Cure be Worse than the Disease?' (presented by Tom Chivers) on 5 May, 2020, epidemiologist and economists debated this question. At the start of the outbreak, the leading researcher of the former science at Imperial College, London, Professor Neil Ferguson, had predicted that hundreds of thousands would die in the UK if the disease was unchecked, and his influence on the government was pivotal in the lock-down decision. Looking back at this decision, Philip Thomas, Professor of Risk Management, suggested that any meaningful comparison between these alternatives involved comparing lives with lives; if the economy contracted by more than 6.4 per cent, more lives would be lost through this decline of income among poor people than would have been in the pandemic. By then a fall of double this amount was predicted. Emily Jackson, Professor of Medical Law, said that more people would die from unemployment and social isolation than from the virus. There were differences between the views of philosophers over the ethics of whether all lives should be seen as of equal value, or whether those of younger people should be given priority over those already in poor health and of a great age.

Issues of social value were explicitly debated by economists and insurance experts in a programme the following day, 'How to Value a Human Life' (BBC Radio 4, 6 May, 2020). Experiences such as terrorist atrocities had given rise to insurance claims requiring values to be put on the lives of victims with a variety of educational qualifications, work experiences and recent earnings profiles, as well as ages and health histories. In decisions over public funding for medical research, trade-offs over pain relief and length of probable survival were made. But it was agreed that the coronavirus situation was unique, because it involved something like 'the fate of humanity', almost in the same category as climate change, and the value of the relationships at stake was extremely difficult to assess. There was also the question of how to compare the value of life in a poor country with one in an affluent society.

All these issues, which are very seldom debated in 'normal' times, have been made urgent ones by the pandemic. Social control and risk management are related in complex ways. The pandemic saw unprecedented levels of controls, which would otherwise have been unacceptable in liberal democracies in peace time, being rolled out in all these societies, with only fairly minor variations, seemingly not related to the political character of their governments. The kinds of issues which pre-occupied sociologists in the 1970s seemed very remote in this situation, with the virus more akin to an alien invasion or armed foe at the border than any ordinary threat to the health of the population.

The paradox of the pandemic was that, as social control became more explicit and obvious, it also became more acceptable, and even welcome. In this sense, it was very like the war-time controls enforced by the UK government, which did nothing to diminish the morale of the population. But this was not obvious in the early months of conflict, as the German Army's breakthrough led to the British retreat to Dunkirk, awaiting the flotilla of 'little ships' to take them across the Channel.

In the film *Darkest Hour* (directed by Joe Wright, 2017), the newly appointed Prime Minister, Winston Churchill (played by Gary Oldman), who had been in the political wilderness for many years, and whose return to the Cabinet had been marked by a disastrous attempt to invade Nazi-controlled Norway, is shown facing an agonising decision over whether to attempt a deal with Hitler, in order to stave off an invasion. He faces strong pressure from his immediate predecessor, Neville Chamberlain, and his Foreign Minister, Lord Halifax, to enlist Mussolini's Italy to help negotiate the truce. He lacks support in his own party, or from the Labour opposition.

In the film, Churchill impulsively leaps from a taxi taking him to Parliament, and boards a tube train (for the first time in his life). Recognised by the (working-class) passengers, he consults them about his dilemma; they are unanimous in supporting defiance. As he enters Parliament, the news comes through that Hitler is intransigent regardless. He makes his famous speech, inspiring all but the two best-known appeasers to cheering resistance, and creates the basis for the war-time coalition government.

In this moment of crisis, the nature of social value in British society during the war was redefined. Instead of deriving from love of peace with other nations, it consisted in stoical survival and solidarity, against all odds. Citizens, including the royal family, suffered and endured without complaint, in a community of common interest.

In most other situations, social controls are either disguised or applied only to those least able to resist them in overt ways. It is only in crises such as pandemics and wars that they are accepted without complaint, because of an external threat of real gravity. The coronavirus pandemic is unlikely to make current controls acceptable for the length of time (more than five years) that rationing of many consumer items lasted after the Second World War. The media were already pressuring for relaxation of many of these measures by the end of May, 2020.

References

Becker, H. S. (1974). Labelling Theory Reconsidered. In *Outsiders*. New York: Free Press.

Foucault, M. (1975). Discipline and Punish. In P. Rabinow (Ed.), *The Foucault Reader: An Introduction to Foucault's Thought*. London: Penguin (1984).

Jordan, B. (1996). *A Theory of Poverty and Social Exclusion*. Cambridge: Polity (Republished by Rawat Publications, New Delhi, 2015).

Jordan, B., James, S., Redley, M., & Kay, H. (1992). *Trapped in Poverty? Labour-Market Decisions in Low-Income Families*. London: Routledge.

Marcuse, H. (1969). *Essay on Liberation*. London: Penguin.

Young, J. (1971). *The Drug-Takers: The Social Meaning of Drug Use*. London: Paladin.

Zuboff, S. (2019). *The Age of Surveillance Capitalism and the Fight for a Human Future at the Frontier of Power*. New York: Profile Books.

CHAPTER 5

The Dynamics of Social Value

Abstract If social value is created in relationships, how does this occur? Do exchanges of intimacy, friendship and association give rise to the same kinds of value, or different ones? Are all of them equally important for the well-being of societies? How do radical changes in organisation and structure come about? These are some of the questions which will be addressed in this chapter.

Keywords Institutions • Culture • Risk • Sustainability

The term 'Subjective Well-being' was adopted by social scientists from the early 1970s onwards to indicate a quantifiable measure of human experience which could counterbalance the 'welfare' in terms of which economists analysed collective goods and public services. In the same decade, the latter category had been re-theorised in terms of individual choices rather than government policies by economists like Buchanan (1968), Olson (1965, 1982) and Oates (1972), who insisted that the principles of liberal democracy and free markets demanded that citizens should be able to choose the quantity and quality of their collective services, and that this could be achieved if they were enabled to pay different amounts in contributions for each of these goods according to their needs and resources.

B. Jordan, *Social Value in Public Policy*,
https://doi.org/10.1007/978-3-030-60421-9_5

Although no state adopted the radical form in which these ideas were presented, all (including the former Soviet Bloc countries) were influenced by them in the final two decades of the century. Programmes for 'privatising' the public sectors of these polities were widely adopted, and better-off citizens soon received education and health care which was of a much better standard than their impoverished fellow-citizens, even when these services had not been privatised. This was because, as earnings became more unequal, the residential districts of the better-off attracted the best teachers, doctors and other professionals to their facilities, while the most deprived ones had services more focused on social control (see Chap. 4).

In the UK, better-off households described themselves as focused on giving their children the best chance in life, some using this to justify sending them to private schools, and enlisting them in many out-of-school activities (Jordan et al. 1994), while those living in the poorest districts justified practices like doing paid work while claiming unemployment-related benefits by saying that it was the only way to compensate for unfair disadvantages (Jordan et al. 1992).

In this chapter, I shall consider how the analysis of social value addresses transformations such as this one, which involved the replacement of one set of institutions, and the attitudes and decisions made within them, by another. It may well be that we are currently experiencing a transformation as profound as that which happened in the 1980s, not because of a revolution in economic theory and a radical shift in the ideology of governments, but as a result of the impact of the coronavirus.

After all, it would not be the first time that pestilence had caused such a radical shift. In the fourteenth century, a rural English economy which had been largely unchanged since the Norman conquest was transformed by a series of waves of bubonic plague, both allowing the feudal peasants to gain access to their own plots of land, and accelerating the drift into towns and cities (BBC 4TV, 'The English Middle Ages', 6 May, 2020). This was arguably the key to the individualistic political culture that characterised England for the rest of its subsequent history (Macfarlane 1976).

Although the coronavirus caused a tiny proportion of deaths compared with the Black Death, the suspension of so much economic activity over a period of months did cause a fall in national income of around 15 per cent in a single month (April, 2020), and involved the state in a range of interventions which were without parallel in peace time. This meant that relationships with officials and fellow-citizens became far more prominent sources of well-being (or survival), and the plight of the most vulnerable (such as care home residents) far more a matter for general concern.

In other words, well-being that arose from material gains was of less account, and that which arose from relationships (whether with kin, neighbours or strangers) became – as in war-time – more significant. Conventional measurement of well-being does only partial justice to this kind of shift, in which an overall sense of what makes life meaningful is refocused on a different set of common purposes, shared in different ways, involving new kinds of bonds with others.

Conflicting Priorities

Although survival through lock-down to the resumption of 'normal' life was the focus of media attention, this was not the way many people experienced the pandemic's impact. Rather it was an intensification of the sense of the collective, at every level. Although intimacy and association, often difficult to express, remained very important, *belonging* gained increased significance.

These new features of the cultural landscape took shape against a background of official responses to the pandemic which were often inept and bungling. Although the UK government had huge stocks of personal protective equipment (PPE) in warehouses, it emerged that a very high percentage of these had passed the date at which they could be safely deployed; this was not admitted until long after the death rate had reached its peak, but as the rate in care homes (still inadequately supplied with PPE) was still rising (Channel 4, *News*, 7th May, 2020).

This confusion was not entirely due to political incompetence; the experts themselves were often uncertain of the best way to proceed. One Oxford University epidemiologist offered the opinion that about half the population had already had the virus, so it was not so deadly after all (BBC Radio 4, 'A Cure, But at What Cost?' presented by Tom Chivers, 5 May, 2020). Philip Thomas, Professor of Risk Management, said that it was a question of evaluating how much risk cost in terms of lives saved. If the economy contracted by more than 6.4 per cent, then more lives would be lost through poverty and its effects than if the virus had been allowed to spread; this view was echoed by Emily Jackson, Professor of Medical Law at the London School of Economics, who pointed out the consequences of unemployment and isolation on mental health. The epidemiologist George Davey-Smith said that the data was still too unreliable to predict outcomes. Philosophers argued about whether lives should always be taken to be of equal value, or whether some measure of quality of life should be factored into any calculation – for instance, should prolonging a life in severe pain be considered desirable.

Jonathan Portas, who had advised Gordon Brown, the Prime Minister during the financial crisis of 2008–9, said that the government should not worry about the fiscal deficit in the long term, and that priority should be given to preparing the NHS for a future crisis. It was pointed out that interest rates were historically low, so borrowing was relatively inexpensive.

But at this time there were additional issues of social justice. Another cause for concern was the fact that, even after adjustments to allow for various factors which inflated the discrepancy, Black and Minority Ethnic staff in the NHS and care homes, and citizens, were twice as likely to die of the virus as white residents. Similar discrepancies were announced in the USA, suggesting that there might be a genetic explanation for these figures.

Local Projects for Sustainability

The social value of projects for sustainability is among the potential gains from the coronavirus that has come with the experience of lock-down. Opportunities to do more rural walks, spend more time gardening and simply appreciate the benefits of clean air constitute potential sources of change for the period immediately after restrictions on mobility, economic activity and other interactions end.

Although China is responsible for one third of the world's emissions of carbon dioxide, and is unlikely to cut these in the near future, both the European Union countries and the Democratic Party candidate for the US presidency, Joe Biden, plan to spend billions on 'green deals' for renewable energy, new infrastructure (such as charging points) for electric vehicles and cleaner public transport systems (BBC Radio 4, 'Today', 25 May, 2020).

But the change in this direction has also been evident at the local level, and it is here that projects for sustainability also contribute most to social value, through the relationships between participants. For example, the town of Frome in Somerset, UK, has been transformed through a movement started by a local citizen, previously inexperienced in politics or environmentalism, Peter MacFaddyen. The local authority is the parish council, and had been concerned previously only with parks, bus stops and traffic control. From his previous experience (as a gardener, disability rights worker and employee of voluntary organisations in Africa and India) he was struck by the lack of participation in local democracy in the town (BBC Radio 4, 'The Spark', presented by Helen Lewis, 25 May, 2020).

In spite of his lack of previous political experience (he had never been a member of a party), MacFaddyen contacted others (only one of whom, a former Chief Executive of the council, had previously been involved in local issues), to form a new Independent Party; it took all the seats on the parish council contested in 2017 and 2019. His party had no manifesto, and no system of discipline, insisting on informality, to the point of members sitting among the public at meetings. By making issues more accessible, posters more informal and cartoon-like, and floating 'whacky ideas', there was an increase of some 75 per cent in polling in the town.

More ambitiously, the council borrowed £250,000 to buy the disused town hall as a local community hub, and another £750,000 to renovate it; yet the local part of the council tax was increased by no more than £7 a year, because of low interest rates. The party sustained constant participation and engagement with citizens. MacFaddyen stepped down as leader in 2019, to campaign for these policies elsewhere: 100 towns in the UK came to have significant independent representation, and there was interest in the story from Finland, Queensland, Australia and New Zealand. Several towns near Buckfastleigh in Devon collaborated to set up similar schemes, with active participation by a voluntary sector, substantially subsidised by the council.

There is no direct evidence of increases in well-being, and hence social value, from projects such as these, but it is difficult to believe that these did not occur. At worst, they represented a direct challenge to the authoritarian alternatives which present themselves in the aftermath of the pandemic and the consequent economic recession.

Conclusions

As populations emerge from lock-down, the redundancies caused by closures of businesses in hospitality, the performance arts and tourism will create a potential workforce for environmental projects. If these can be creatively and imaginatively managed, they might compensate for the loss of social value in the service sector, and contribute to long-term improvements in quality of life.

Awareness of these factors, and of their relevance for social value, has certainly risen during lock-down. As part of an overall re-evaluation which has occurred during this period, as people have time to reflect, and become more conscious of their mortality, they may have come to give higher priority to these aspects of sustainability.

But this can only be achieved by reversing the strong trend towards authoritarianism in government. Most notably President Bolsonaro in Brazil but also President Trump have shown a lack of concern for environmental destruction alongside their disregard for liberal rights and values. The politics of social value will have to win over those who supported them (often because they themselves felt devalued by the economic consequences of globalisation) in order to change this direction in policies.

References

Buchanan, J. M. (1968). *The Demand and Supply of Public Goods.* Chicago: Rand McNally.

Jordan, B., James, S., Redley, M., & Kay, H. (1992). *Trapped in Poverty? Labour-Market Decisions in Low-Income Households.* London: Routledge.

Jordan, B., Redley, M., & James, S. (1994). *Putting the Family First: Identities, Decisions, Citizenship.* London: UCL Press.

Macfarlane, A. (1976). *The Origins of English Individualism: The Family, Property and Social Transition.* Oxford: Blackwell.

Oates, W. E. (1972). *Fiscal Federalism.* New York: Harcourt Brace Jovanovich.

Olson, M. (1965). *The Logic of Collective Action: Public Goods and the Economics of Groups.* Cambridge, MA: Harvard University Press.

Olson, M. (1982). *The Rise and Decline of Nations: Economic Growth, Stagflation and Social Rigidities.* New Haven: Yale University Press.

CHAPTER 6

The Value of Care

Abstract During the coronavirus pandemic in the UK, attention increasingly focused on the death rate of elderly and disabled residents in care homes, as well as the staff. On 29 April, 2020, the news came that deaths the previous week in these institutions – far more dispersed and numerous than those of the NHS – had exceeded those in the latter's hospitals. Although it had been clear from the first stages of the pandemic that older people with established preconditions were far more vulnerable to its impact than young, physically fit people, it was shocking that those who could do nothing to safeguard themselves through isolation were supplying the virus with concentrations of easy victims in this way. Furthermore, the high proportions of Black, Asian and minority ethnic staff in these homes, and their lack of personal protective equipment, made them doubly vulnerable to the virus.

Keywords Vulnerability • Older people • Residential care • Black Lives Matter

The care home residents were from the generation which had fought, suffered and survived the Second World War, yet they were now being exposed once more to the highest risks in the face of a new deadly hazard. Furthermore, residential care, and services for elderly and disabled people in the community, represented the longest-running unresolved policy

B. Jordan, *Social Value in Public Policy*,
https://doi.org/10.1007/978-3-030-60421-9_6

issue in the social services in the UK. It was a reproach to the democratic process that, despite repeated pledges by the political parties, and the availability of examples of the same issues being eventually negotiated and resolved in other European countries, the evidence of the harm to this generation's well-being due to these failures was now clear in grim statistics.

There were many reasons why this situation had been allowed to develop. Perhaps the most fundamental was that the historical mode of care for those older people who survived past pandemics and the hazards of working life involved women's roles in extended family households. For instance, at the time of the Spanish Flu of 1919, women's participation rate was around 35 per cent, and during the peace that followed until 1939 it remained roughly stable. Overall, service jobs (including domestic service, which made up around a third of their employment) grew by 33 per cent, as manufacturing work, mainly by men, fell by 3 per cent between 1920 and 1938 (Feinstein 1976, Table 59, p. 129). Women played a crucial role during the Second World War, but then resumed household roles in large numbers when peace came. In the 1960s, they were catching up with developments in Sweden, but ahead of those in Germany; between 1951 and 2018, the total figures for economically active women increased from seven to over 15 million (Office for National Statistics, *Labour Force Survey*, 2019).

The contraction in industrial employment and the growth in service work were key factors, but many of the new employments were part-time, and women's earnings were supplementary to those of their partners (Pahl 1984). The political parties were slow to recognise that, as life expectancy increased, women were bearing the heaviest burdens, as carers for their parents as well as their children, in addition to their roles as contributors to household earnings. In Britain in 1983, 5 per cent of all men and 15 per cent of all women over 80 were being looked after in their children's households (OPCS, *General Household Survey*, 1983, Table 3.7, p. 15). But the supply of family carers was declining; at that time it was already forecast that the average couple in their 80s, which had 40 surviving female relatives, would have only 11 when reaching that age in 2000 (Ermisch 1983, p. 283).

This prospect was recognised by the political parties, but other priorities always supervened. Following the White Paper '*Caring for People*' (1989) and the NHS and Community Care Act (1990), local authority care services had been re-organised and contracted out to private companies. But also because of the low status of work in care homes, and the fact that most of the electorate had little contact with this sector except at the end of their elders' lives, the issue did not command much priority. The establishment of a truly national system of care, on a par with the NHS, and directly funded from taxation or social insurance contributions, in line with Continental developments, was seen as unlikely to pay electoral dividends.

The coronavirus pandemic exposed the weaknesses in care systems in a tragic way. By 29 April, 2020, deaths in UK residential homes exceeded those in NHS hospitals (Channel 4 TV, 'News'). There was too little testing for the virus, and too little PPE, and what there was came too late, as staff and residents succumbed. The huge number of homes, dispersed all over the country, many in isolated rural locations, made them less accessible for these protective measures than they were for the virus.

Looking back on these tragedies two months later, the Chief Executive of one group, Goldcare Homes, where 169 residents had died, said that there would have to be closures of some of his facilities, because of low occupancy, a fall in admissions and loss of income – numbers of self-funding residents in particular had fallen. One report said that county councils were building their own homes for the first time since the 1980s. The government was giving £3.2 billion in support for the sector, and £600 million for measures to prevent infection. The report recommended higher minimum wages for care workers, and better training and status, in recognition of their heroism and sacrifices during the pandemic (BBC Radio 4, 'You and Yours', presented by Winifred Robinson, 18 June, 2020).

These tragedies were not confined to the UK. At the end of April, 2020, it was reported that there had been 20,000 deaths in Spain's residential homes since early March, over half their populations. The loss of life was initially covered up by the government, but broke in the press because of disclosures by relatives of residents at the Montermoso home, a four-storey 120-bed facility on the outskirts of Madrid, which also provided day care for the district's needs. The home stopped responding to relatives' telephone calls on 17 March, when the national lock-down had just started, by which time 46 were dead. Ambulances refused to visit the home, and the funeral company was causing delays in collecting the bodies. When the military arrived, there were many dead bodies in the rooms which they had been sent to disinfect.

In one case, an elderly couple had gone on sharing a room for six days after the wife became ill; she died on 16 March, after having been refused admission to the local hospital. An Alzheimer's Disease sufferer, her husband was holding her hand at the moment of her death. By then some 65 residents had symptoms of the virus, as attention of politicians and the media focused on hospitals; care staff and residents in homes lacked PPE. The virus was rumoured to have come to Spain through a man who had been skiing in the Alps, and the delay in publicity about the plight of care home staff and residents (in contrast to hospital patients) was attributed to the insecurity of the non-unionised status of the former workers and the power of private home-owners (BBC Radio 4, 'Crossing Continents', 'Spain's Care Home Nightmare', presented by Linda Presley, 30 April).

One of the surprising features of statistics on SWB is the fact that – in the advanced capitalist democracies – older people have the highest levels of well-being. This may reflect the fact that their citizenship status and rights are the least contested in the age groups. Retirement pensions – historically the first to be granted in liberal democracies, and the least conditional – have tended to be more generous than benefits for other age groups, as well as largely unconditional. If media stereotypes of older people are often insultingly patronising, at least they do not present them as dangerous deviants. The popular press and TV channels are constantly on the look-out for old people who – like the Second World War veteran Captain Tom Moore – are courageously battling ill-health to perform unlikely feats such as walking for many miles to raise money for charities, even on their hundredth birthday (BBC Radio 4, 'Today', 30 April, 2020).

So, whereas the public provision of care for children raises a whole series of hotly disputed issues (over the state's capacities and duties to support and police parenting, to socialise young people, and to supply substitute families for those who lack suitable ones in which to grow up), both income maintenance and care for older citizens have historically been much less disputed fields for policy. But there are still important questions about how services can bestow the highest levels of social value on their ways of life.

For instance, as work (including much service work) becomes more automated, should this allow earlier 'retirement' from the labour market, or should people work fewer hours per week over a longer period? Should we see residential care as a 'last resort', or could it be transformed into a way of life with more social value than a potentially isolated experience at home? And if the UBI becomes available for people of working age, should there be a different system of income maintenance beyond a certain age, or should older people be part of the same tax-benefit regime as younger ones? These questions will be explored in the final two chapters.

The Genesis of the Problems

The underlying issue for this field in social policy was the growth in the numbers and proportion of the UK population aged 70 and over. Between 2008–9 and 2018–19, those in England aged 65–74 increased by 21 per cent, aged 75–85 by 14 per cent, and aged over 85 by 20 per cent. Of all those over 80, 44 per cent needed some kind of help with daily life. Meanwhile policies for de-institutionalisation in the fields of mental illness and mental handicap had led to the establishment of large numbers of small-to-medium-sized units in communities, some run by local authorities, others by private providers. Many residents were older people.

Under New Labour, a White Paper on services for adults (Department of Health 1998) had criticised local authorities for failing to support people with disabilities and chronic illnesses in their homes. The personal social services had for some time been shown to have difficulties in meshing with family and neighbourhood networks of support for older people (Finch and Groves 1984). Research by Challis and Davies (1985) had shown that lack of flexible and intensive packages of home care had caused unnecessary admissions to residential homes – an experience which the sociologists Miller and Gwynne (1972) had characterised as 'social death'.

However, it took a number of scandals and deaths of care residents for the system to be reformed. Under the 1990 Act, 90 per cent of care provision was to be in privately owned homes, rather than ones owned by local authorities. Between 1980 and 2001 the proportion of residents in private homes rose from 18 to 85 per cent; by 2005 it was 90 per cent (Johnson et al. 2010, p. 236). A number of companies owning such homes went bankrupt in the financial crash of 2008–9, but by far the most notorious such collapse was that of Southern Cross in 2011.

At the start of that year, Southern Cross owned 750 care homes all over Britain, employing 44,000 staff and accommodating 31,000 residents, of whom about 70 per cent were funded by local authorities. In the North East of England they were providing 30 per cent of all care home beds (House of Commons Public Accounts Committee 2011). But this situation represented the outcome of a frenzied round of transactions which had little to do with the well-being of frail elderly people, and a great deal to do with financial capitalism.

In September, 2004, the New York-based equity giant Blackstone had acquired Darlington-based Southern Cross Healthcare, a company with New Zealand origins, for £162 million, which had previously been owned by a similar firm, West Private Equity, for two years (Drakeford 2006; Scourfield 2007). Then Blackstone sold off the freeholds of these homes, partly to help finance the purchase of another huge group of private nursing homes, NHP, based in Surrey, which also managed another 165 homes through its subsidiary company, Highfield Care.

These transactions were motivated entirely by profit; Blackstone simultaneously bought a German chemicals company, the Dutch telephone directory supplier VNU, and a French cinema group. By this stage, care homes had become commodities to be traded, with little regard for the well-being of their residents. Because Southern Cross had sold the freeholds of its homes, it was vulnerable at the onset of the 2008–9 financial crash, because it was paying rents for the land on which they stood, which by 2011 had risen by 18.6 per cent in a period when property values were falling; these totalled £250 million a year, to 80 different landlords, including two banks which had been nationalised during the crash. Southern Cross posted half-year losses of £311 million in May, 2011, and a month later it ceased to exist (Jordan and Drakeford 2012, pp. 88–91).

This was by no means an isolated example. In the wake of these events, it emerged that Qatari Investment Authority, one of the largest owners of that group's freeholds, was a company registered in the Cayman Islands, a tax haven. One of the largest new owners of Southern Cross's chain was a new company, NHP, whose founder, Dr Chai Patel, had been chief executive of Westminster Healthcare when a resident of one of its homes, Lynde House, had been neglected and mistreated, a scandal exposed by the London *Evening Standard*. Another set of questionable financial transactions surrounded the Four Seasons group of homes, where suspiciously high rates of profit appeared in their accounts of October, 2011 (GMB 2011).

What all the cases illustrated was that 'care' – nominally a set of relationships through which the social value is expressed in looking after the most vulnerable and dependent members of the population – had become detached from the task of maximising their well-being, and was instead organised around gains through financial trading. Once again, the tensions between relationships appropriate for emotional flourishing (or at very least, a life without emotional suffering), and the competition for material wealth, had put at risk the former for the sake of the latter.

Furthermore, and of even more concern in many ways, it became clear in mid-May that the NHS had looked after its own professional and institutional interests at the expense of the care system. By the second week of April, 40 per cent of deaths in England had been in care homes. Advice had been given by government, which remained uncontradicted between mid-February and mid-March, that there was no risk of a coronavirus outbreak in care homes, in spite of warnings in previous years to local authorities that the sector was vulnerable to such infections; the new evidence was that 10,000 more deaths than in previous years occurred during this month. A payment of £600 million for infection control to the care sector was very belated; local council finances were in crisis, with a £10 billion gap in their funds (BBC Radio 4, 'Today', 14 May, 2020).

As the low priority given to this sector received critical attention in the media, the fact that many care staff, especially in London, were from ethnic minority backgrounds, and that they seemed more vulnerable to the fatal effects of the coronavirus, was also made more prominent. This connected with the outrage about the police killing of George Floyd in the USA, and the rise of the Black Lives Matter movement in the UK also, to form the focus of protest mobilisations (see Chap. 7).

Revaluing Older People and Their Care

Older people are a group in societies whose well-being is most fragile; they are vulnerable to illnesses and accidents at the best of times, and the coronavirus pandemic made them doubly so. Under normal circumstances in the UK, they could expect to receive domiciliary support, especially if they lived alone, both during illnesses and after a period in hospital, and as their mobility declined.

But the residential care (which normally marked their transition to dependence on a more intensive form of practical assistance) was usually seen as supplying a form of security, after a process of growing risk (from falls, or the loss of sight, for instance). Suddenly, being in a care home meant exposure to the highest risk to health and life itself, with the onset of the pandemic.

Furthermore, hospitals now had incentives to discharge such patients as fast as possible, to keep their own rates of infection from Covid-19 down. This added to the vulnerability of the residents of care homes.

The real reason, surely, why social care had not been integrated within the NHS in the UK was that the medical profession was unwilling to be seen to accept as a full partner something as unprestigious as practical help for people with Alzheimer's disease or mental or physical disabilities. Care continued to be seen as an adjunct to medicine which was concerned with residual tasks, once every remedial procedure had been performed.

The price for these hierarchical assumptions was paid during the coronavirus pandemic. There continued to be thousands of dispersed care homes, owned by private firms, many with only a few establishments; they were underfunded, and some were understaffed. As the hospitals filled up with victims of the pandemic, there was soon a drastic shortage of places for those older patients cured of it to be discharged for the further care they needed. There is now evidence that patients (both those with other conditions and those who had been suffering with coronavirus symptoms) were discharged to care homes before they had been adequately tested (BBC Radio 4, 'PM', 13 May, 2020). Soon deaths in care homes exceeded those in hospitals; the number of deaths in care homes from mid-April to early May was three times the average number of previous years, while those in hospitals were lower than the average for that time of year (ibid.).

Then the virus itself began to infect the homes; once it penetrated them, it spread like wild-fire among residents and staff. In this emergency, some homes resorted to a system by which the staff decided to lock down with the residents, to avoid bringing in the virus or taking it home (BBC Radio 4, 'Today', 30 April). This decision indicated a dedication and commitment by staff which did much to expunge the notoriety associated with the homes during the financial manipulation at the start of the decade.

As nothing else in the long and indecisive debate about the future status of care had done, the pandemic focused on the need for a fundamental overhaul of the system. It was a national scandal that care homes had become the most unsafe environments in the UK for citizens to find themselves; but it indicated the consequences of decades of indecision and postponement in this field of social policy.

As I have argued throughout this book, interpersonal relationships involve the creation and exchange of social value, but these processes are vulnerable to the corrosive effects of economic, power and criminal forces. Services such as the care of elderly, chronically ill and disabled people are especially vulnerable to these influences, because the decision to enter residential facilities usually follows a long and painful chain of events, in which family or other informal care has broken down. Very often this arises from the illness of the person most involved in care-giving, and it can happen even after much support from domiciliary services has been received over a prolonged period (Jordan with Jordan 2000, pp. 89–95).

Although the finance of care has been an unresolved problem for many decades (Dilnot Commission 2011), the machinations of the very large care home owners who use them as a source for various kinds of international property deals and tax-avoidance scams should not obscure the vital role of this work in an age of increased life expectancy. As the coronavirus pandemic has reminded everyone, some of the citizens who have been losing their lives to the Covid-19 virus are the people who defended liberal democracy against totalitarianism in their early adult lives, and who surely deserve better.

Currently, life expectancy for men of working age in the USA is falling. The causes of death which are bringing this about include obesity, alcohol and drug abuse and suicide; the highest rates are in rustbelt former industrial areas with high unemployment (BBC Radio 4, 'News', 27 November, 2019). In the UK, it is the life expectancy of working-class women that is falling. In each case, this seems to be one of the consequences of greater inequalities in their societies.

The insurance industry has high-status lawyers and economists concerned with placing a financial value on human lives. This became the focus of attention as a result of the random deaths of victims of terrorism, such as the 9/11 attack in New York. Some of these were stockbrokers and bankers, others maintenance workers or passers-by in the street below. In a radio broadcast (BBC Radio 4, 'How to Value a Human Life', 6 May, 2020), the lawyer Ken Feinberg said that the estimate of what one person could earn in a lifetime varied between $750 million for a stockbroker and $850 thousand for an undocumented immigrant waiter. Emotional loss was measured in standard amounts – $250 thousand for a spouse, $150 thousand for each surviving child. But survivors reported that the process of claiming for physical and psychological suffering and the costs of treatment felt like begging, not a right.

Parallel with this, the UK committee evaluating whether the NHS should purchase a new drug, NICE, used the concept of QUALYs (Quality-Adjusted Life-Years) to reach their decisions. Thus they applied a trade-off to their decisions: length of life versus pain and suffering. But the value of relationships was not included (Institute of Government 2019). The coronavirus is a new challenge, since millions of lives, and possibly even the 'fate of humanity', appeared to be at stake – more like climate change than a normal illness or accident, though perhaps comparable with the impact of a typhoon or tsunami.

On 29 April, 2020, cancer experts predicted an extra 18,000 extra deaths from this disease being untreated in the UK because of the priority for pandemic victims, but in reality the power of the medical profession ensured a very different outcome. In the second week of April, 40 per cent of all coronavirus deaths were in care homes. By the middle of May, the death rate in care homes in the UK was greater than that in hospitals.

It had become clear that the government had mishandled the issue from the start. Questions in the House of Commons in mid-May revealed that for a month from mid-February, the government had advised that there was no risk of an outbreak in the care sector. Hospital patients were not tested for Covid-19 before being transferred to care homes. In the event, care home deaths were 10,000 more than the average for previous years during these months. The care sector had just been given a belated extra £600 million for emergency measures (BBC Radio 4, 'Today', 14 May).

Conclusions

The neglect of the sector over decades was reflected in these appalling statistics, in which care workers as well as elderly and disabled residents were victims. The Chair of the National Care Association said in retrospect that the sector had been used to protect the NHS, and staff felt completely abandoned; the government had been badly advised. Visitors were allowed long after this was obviously risky (BBC Radio 4, 'Today', 14 May, 2020). It was in this sector that the impact of Covid-19 most closely resembled a major natural disaster; the post-pandemic policy landscape, already crowded with urgent issues, should surely include this one as a high priority in the aftermath.

Meanwhile, the NHS was struggling to balance its response to the coronavirus with its other main priorities. Partly because of fears by patients about self-referral in a period of pandemic, investigations of suspected cancer fell sharply, along with those for suspected heart and lung problems. Numbers of patients arriving at Accident and Emergency Departments of hospitals fell to half the usual figures. While some of this was due to the fall in traffic accidents on the much emptier roads, it also indicated some concern by citizens not to overtax the services in this period of crisis (BBC Radio 4, 'World at One', 14 May, 2020).

Solidarity, expressed in applause for the NHS each Thursday evening, was transferred to the care sector as the extent of mortality in residential care was revealed, and a time to express support was allotted. But it was symbolic of the differentiation of status between cure and care that this was far less widely observed.

The tragic toll of deaths in care homes has reminded the UK electorate of how long a period has elapsed since their re-organisation and upgrading was first mooted. But these more fundamental issues of social value in services have not all been made explicit. The origins of some of these and other omissions will be considered in the next chapter.

References

Challis, D., & Davies, B. (1985). *Long-Term Care of the Elderly: The Community Care Scheme.* Discussion Paper 386. Canterbury: Personal Social Services Research Unit, University of Kent.

Department of Health. (1989). *Caring for People; Community Care in the Next Decade and Beyond.* London: Department of Health/HMSO.

Department of Health. (1998). *Modernising Social Services: Promoting Independence, Improving Protection, Raising Standards,* Cm. 4169. London: Department of Health/HMSO.

Dilnot Commission. (2011). *Fairer Funding for All: Report of the Commission on Funding for Care and Support.* London: Department of Health.

Drakeford, M. (2006). Ownership, Regulation and the Public Interest: The Case of Residential Care for Older People. *Critical Social Policy, 26*(4), 932–944.

Ermisch, J. (1983). *The Political Economy of Demographic Change.* London: Heinemann.

Feinstein, C. H. (1976). *Statistical Tables of National Income, Expenditure and Output of the UK, 1855–1965.* Cambridge: Cambridge University Press.

Finch, J., & Groves, D. (1984). *Labour of Love.* London: Allen and Unwin.

GMB. (2011, October 4). *Four Seasons Healthcare Accounts for 2010: How Earnings (EBITARM) of £8,408 Per Resident Per Annum to Pay Interest on £790 Million Loans and Rents.*

House of Commons Public Accounts Committee. (2011, December 6). *Report on the Enquiry into the Southern Cross Care Company.*

Institute of Government. (2019). *Adult Social Care.* London: Institute for Government Performance Tracker.

Johnson, J., Rolf, S., & Smith, R. (2010). Uncovering History: Private Care Homes for Older People in England. *Journal of Social Policy, 39*(2), 235–253.

Jordan, B., with Jordan, C. (2000). *Social Work and the Third Way: Tough Love as Social Policy* (pp. 88–93). London: Sage.

Jordan, B., & Drakeford, M. (2012). *Social Work and Social Policy Under Austerity.* Basingstoke: Palgrave Macmillan.

Miller, E. J., & Gwynne, G. V. (1972). *A Life Apart: A Pilot Study of Residential Institutions for Boys*. London: Tavistock Publications.
Office for National Statistics. (2019). *Labour Force Survey*. London: HMSO.
Office of Population Censuses and Surveys. (1983). *General Household Survey*. London: HMSO.
Pahl, R. E. (1984). *Divisions of Labour*. Oxford: Blackwell.
Scourfield, P. (2007). Are there Reasons to Be Worried About the "Cartellisation" of Residential Care? *Critical Social Policy, 25*(2), 255–280.

CHAPTER 7

Class Conflict in the Post-Pandemic World

Abstract When the arrangements for relaxing the lock-down in the UK were announced in mid-May, 2020, the Prime Minister, Boris Johnson, was accused in several newspapers of unleashing a 'class war' against the working class. Factory and transport workers were being encouraged to return to work, and hence were put at risk, while most middle-class jobs could far more readily still be done from home. The rules on child care and social care were unclear, and personal protective equipment was in short supply for both, re-enforcing these injustices (BBC Radio 4, 'Today', 12 May, 2020). The Black Lives Matter movement, a mass mobilisation which followed the killing of George Floyd by a white policeman in Minneapolis, USA, quickly led to large demonstrations and marches for the same cause in the UK.

Keywords Racism • Income support • Furlough • Social justice

The day before Boris Johnson's announcement, it had been reported that bus drivers, security guards and chefs were over four times more likely than the average citizen of working age to die from the coronavirus. Other working-class jobs were twice as susceptible to infections leading to fatalities. By contrast, hospital professionals' death rates were no higher than the average.

B. Jordan, *Social Value in Public Policy*,
https://doi.org/10.1007/978-3-030-60421-9_7

In the years leading up to the pandemic, class seemed to be becoming a less prominent factor in electoral politics. Many blue-collar workers had voted for Donald Trump, especially those from rustbelt states where de-industrialisation had been most extensive. The North of England had voted Conservative in far higher numbers in December, 2019, than in any other election in the decade. But, above all, social democratic parties seemed to be on the retreat all over Europe, with the UK Labour Party just one example of many (Wales was an exception, with Mark Drakeford becoming the only Labour First Minister).

In France, Emmanuel Macron's *En Marche* and the *Front National* had drawn members away from the Socialist Party to such an extent that in mid-May, 2020, its leaders decided to approach the Greens to propose a merger – from a position of weakness, not strength. In Germany, the Social Democrats were in scarcely better shape, in the face of the rise in support for the far-right *Alternative für Deutschland* and the Greens.

In the USA, the politics of race and racism have always been an underlying theme of all responses to and outcomes of crises, such as the pandemic; to be both poor and Black represents double jeopardy. The country's rate of infection comprised 25 per cent of global totals, with Black and minority ethnic people three times as likely as their white fellow-citizens to be among these, and nearly twice as likely to die in consequence (Emily Tamkin, 'Inside America: How Trump Uses the Culture Wars as a Distraction from the Accelerating Covid-19 Crisis', *New Statesman* (10–16 July, 2020, p. 21).

It should have been clear that class issues have never gone away; the differential rates of fatalities from coronavirus were only revealing what should have continued to be obvious. The factor which concealed them was that the working class had become divided by the processes of de-industrialisation all over the West, and the policies for wage supplementation of the less favoured service workers which had caused this.

There was also a resurgence of far right activism in the UK, including mobilisation by young people. The internet allowed this neo-Nazi movement to publish its violent views, including celebrating the murder of Labour MP Jo Cox. This appears to have been part of an international network, sponsoring acts of terrorism from Russia to the USA. They trained their recruits to 'shed empathy' and enjoy sadism, and formed an increasing part of the workload of MI5, the security service, attacking Jews, Muslims, women and BAME citizens (BBC Radio 4, 'File on Four', 'Extreme Right', presented by Daniel Day Simeone, 28 June, 2020).

But in the wider context of British society, the pandemic had knitted together a divided working class. In a very paradoxical way, the need to supplement the incomes of *all* (or most) members of the working class had reunited it, and allowed the expression of a common interest, for instance over the risks of re-opening the economy from lock-down.

In principle, this should also have offset the loss in well-being, and hence in social value, of those most at risk of the virus, and of the poverty which accompanied the measures to minimise its spread. Over the long term, the division in the working class had been a major factor in coercive policies which reduced social value; now these were no longer in force. In this chapter, I shall examine the paradoxes in this situation.

The Effects of the Furlough System

The word 'furlough' was almost unknown in British English parlance before the pandemic crisis. It was adopted as a euphemism (or circumlocution), to avoid using any expression which might imply that measures such as the payment of universal (or very widespread) benefits to citizens could be regarded as long-term or permanent rights. If the term meant anything in British English, it suggested a kind of leave of absence, usually applied to sick or injured members of the armed services.

The scheme was originally announced in early May, 2020, as a 'jobs retention' plan, to pay 80 per cent of the wages of those laid off due to the pandemic, up to a maximum of £2500 per month, at a total cost of approximately £40 billion, for four months. With the additional outlay of £10 billion for the self-employed, this amounted to more than the rescue of the banks during the financial crash of 2008–9. Altogether, public borrowing in that crisis had been £100 billion over four years; the pandemic measures would cost an estimated £80 billion over four months (BBC Radio 4, 'The Briefing Room – Prospects for Recovery' (presented by David Aronovitch), 8 May, 2020).

By 12 May, the government was effectively supporting half the UK workforce, and the limited return to work under conditions of safe self-distancing which began then would continue for a further period of several months. But a leaked government document suggested that public borrowing would be ten times as high as had been estimated only four days earlier (BBC Radio 4, 'Today', 13 May, 2020). Later the same day, the Director of the Institute for Fiscal Studies, Paul Johnson, described the fall in national income as 'the recession to end all recessions', an unprecedented decline which might be followed by a rapid recovery, but only if the coronavirus did not break out again, requiring a return to social isolation measures (BBC Radio 4, 'The World at One', 13 May, 2020).

In the same programme, Kenneth Clarke, the Conservative former Chancellor of the Exchequer, said that in an age of nationalism and protectionism, it was very important to achieve international co-operation to stave off the most disastrous economic consequences of the pandemic. DeAnne Julius, former member of the Monetary Committee of the Bank of England, said that, with low interest rates persisting, it should be feasible to increase the fiscal deficit to 10–15 per cent of GDP, and that it would take up to a decade to pay this extra borrowing back. The expert on property sales and values, Kirstie Allsopp, predicted that house prices in rural districts would rise, and those in London's suburbs would fall, as commuters who worked from home during the pandemic discovered that they could find a better quality of life by working from home in the countryside.

Later in the day, Professor of Economics at Cambridge University Diane Coyle said that there was no word in the lexicon of economic terms to describe the extent of the collapse. Health 'output' is likely to fall because of some of the usual tasks foregone; the disruption to the education of the young generation will affect their whole lifetime earnings. In other sectors it is hard to estimate the likely losses through a catastrophic decline in certain key services (BBC Radio 4, 'PM', 13 May, 2020).

In the *New Statesman*, Paul Collier recommended devolution of economic decisions to the regional level (8–14 May, 2020, 'Capitalism after Coronavirus', pp. 25–8), and Simon Jenkins pointed out that the Chancellor was 'measuring lives today against lives tomorrow', with the media holding him to account for his decisions ('The BBC and the Journalism of Fear', pp. 31–2). In general terms, the class component in infection and death rates did not attract as much attention as it perhaps deserved. This may have reflected a kind of loyalty to the NHS as an expression of national solidarity, and the desire not to seem to criticise it.

In this chapter, I shall trace the fluctuations in how the UK polity expressed and managed issues of class and class conflict, and how these influenced welfare and well-being. Much of this story concerned the slow decline of the Liberal Party in the first half of the twentieth century, and the lasting influence of three Liberals, David Lloyd George, J.M. Keynes and Sir William Beveridge, on its public institutions and services.

Defusing Class Conflict

During the nineteenth century, UK governments of both major parties were intensely ambivalent about the participation of the working class in politics. The franchise was very gradually extended (to men, not women), in contrast with the universal suffrage in the USA. But the foundation of the Labour Party at the end of the century signalled a requirement for more active measures to attract votes from workers, through legislation which dealt with the problems most afflicting their lives.

Before this, specific problems of the poor which impacted on the lives of the middle class had been addressed in an ad hoc way. Utilitarians such as Jeremy Bentham, Sir Edwin Chadwick, James Kay-Shuttleworth and Dr Thomas Southwood Smith had campaigned successfully for specific measures for public health and well-being, especially where unsanitary conditions could affect respectable neighbourhoods. For instance, during his long life, Chadwick championed Poor Law reform, the safety of child factory workers, sewers and public health more generally, and these all contributed substantially to the improvement of the lives of urban working-class people. For most of this period, he had been denounced and opposed by these poor people and by the trades unions, but at the end of it (in 1890) he had become popular with those who had reviled him, and their organisations (Finer 1952).

In all these respects, Chadwick (like Bentham) was seen as a suspect anomaly in an age of Liberal *laissez faire*, free-market politics. For instance, he was attacked in *The Times* (3 May, 1833) for 'pomp and pretension combined with…vagueness and apparent insincerity of purpose'. He was denounced as an inquisitor as well as a persecutor of the poor. But what he was really pioneering was a view of society in which the government could steer and influence public behaviour, and thus reduce the need for coercion and punishment. Like one of a new class of benevolent factory-owners, he set about improving the sanitation of the urban environment, providing amenities and making it more attractive, regarding this as 'good economy'. He influenced the growth of an enlarged civil service and local government workforce, with inspectorates to oversee regulations.

But it was not until 1910–11 that a Liberal government enacted legislation to supply a proportion of the workforce with contributory National Insurance benefits for unemployment and sickness, steered through Parliament by the dynamic David Lloyd George and the young (then Liberal) Winston Churchill (Hay 1975). In what turned out to be the swansong of Liberal Britain, the party, relying on support from Irish Home Rulers, responded to a series of damaging strikes in industrial districts and the increase in Labour Party support by measures which penalised the aristocracy, but 'were not designed to advance the worker but to propitiate him' (Dangerfield 1935, p. 32). These were more concerned about diverting attention from the more radical critique of capitalism by the socialists than defending the kind of society which would elect Liberal majorities, 'where social ills would be medicated but never cured; and where the ideal man would come more and more to resemble an honest, tolerant, intolerable grocer' (ibid.).

The Liberal Party never recovered its leading position in British politics after the First World War, yet it did supply the two leading figures in the creation of the welfare state by the end of the Second. John Maynard Keynes was a member of the Bloomsbury Group of novelists, poets and artists, and very much a man of the world; he had contacts with economists all over the Empire and in the USA. His analysis in his highly influential book *A General Theory of Employment, Interest and Money* (1936) was global in its scope, and it became as renowned in the Empire and on the other side of the Atlantic as it had been among politicians in the UK.

He boldly attacked the prevailing economic orthodoxy, that the labour market necessarily and optimally distributed the whole of the 'wages fund' to the whole working class. In reality, he showed, the supply of labour does not necessarily create its own demand, and the economy might reach an equilibrium below full employment because of 'an insufficiency of effective demand'. As a result, the total sum of consumption plus investment could fall short of the levels required to supply jobs for all, especially if the rate of profit declined. In this way, 'deficient effective demand' could lead to 'a level of employment …short of the supply of labour potentially available at the existing wage' (p. 30).

Keynes wanted to construct a theory in which individuals were no longer the constituent units, but was aware that, for most purposes, the whole world was a single economic system (as Adam Smith had recognised); hence an analysis in terms of national units of account was in a sense arbitrary (p. 37), and many of the aggregate terms he coined were 'imprecise and approximate' (p. 43). He was reluctant to propose national policies, and soon moved to the USA, where he presided over the creation of the international monetary system. But his ideas were very influential during the Second World War and the subsequent boom, only to be discredited by the worldwide recession of the 1970s.

Only in the appendices to the *General Theory* did Keynes make specific proposals on policy. His 'Concluding Notes on the Social Philosophy to which the General Theory might Lead' recommended state investment policy, redistribution of income and the 'euthanasia of the rentier', in order to end exploitation of the scarcity-value of capital and land (p. 376). In this way, capitalism could be transformed without a revolution (ibid.); there was no case for state socialism (p. 378). Indeed, the necessary changes could be introduced 'without a break in the general traditions of society' (ibid.).

Sir William Beveridge was a Liberal who had been involved in the reforms of 1908–11, and he was an admirer of Keynes' work; he wanted to make specific its practical and institutional implications, in relation to employment and National Insurance benefits. He supported the idea of managing effective demand, so long as civil liberties could be preserved; the state should protect the population from mass unemployment 'as definitely as it is now the function of the state to defend the citizens against attack from abroad and against robbery and violence at home' (*Full Employment in a Free Society* 1944, p. 29).

If universal secondary education, a National Health Service and family allowances (payments for each child) were available, such an employment policy would supply security against poverty for all but those in certain identifiable circumstances (*Social Insurance and Allied Services* 1942, p. 120). These contingencies formed the basis for Keynes' scheme – non-means-tested flat-rate benefits, funded by compulsory contributions from employers and workers, intended to cover subsistence costs, and leaving claimants to top these up from savings. But the scheme had two great weaknesses: the rates of benefit were already inadequate before it was introduced, and were greatly eroded by inflation over the years that followed; and there was no provision for unsupported women (other than widows), a growing problem as divorce rates increased. Married women received benefits as 'dependants' on their husbands.

This new version of liberalism, implemented by a Labour government, was clearly a sharp divergence from the views of nineteenth-century philosophers such as Herbert Spencer (1860, 1884), whose Social Darwinism constructed poor people as subject to the laws governing the survival of the fittest. But it was still class-based in its institutional regulations. Those without a property income to support them continued to be forced to labour for their subsistence, up to retirement age, in order to qualify for support in times of redundancy, sickness or disability.

Only the National Assistance Board, the heir to the Poor Law authorities, was available to support those who did not qualify for contributory benefits, and it still enforced such relics of the Poor Laws as the 'cohabitation rule', under which women, including those with numerous children, were disqualified from benefit if they were suspected of 'living with' (in effect, having a relationship with) a man.

Meanwhile, a whole class of property-owners had no need for recourse to any of these systems, and from the early 1970s the fortunes of the classes began to diverge more quickly. On the one hand, a larger proportion of the population gained access to higher education, and to jobs with occupational pensions and other perks; they could increasingly afford to borrow money from building societies to purchase their own homes, and to move up the 'housing ladder' as their earnings rose through a career with promotions and bonus payments. On the other, some workers in the increasingly dominant service sector were paid at rates insufficient for subsistence; those with children increasingly required subsidisation through payments (first called Family Income Supplements, later Tax Credits) of means-tested benefits. By 2011, the proportion of workers with families receiving these subsidies was more than 70 per cent.

Conclusions

Since the Second World War, the class structure of British society has been transformed. The de-industrialisation which began in the mid-1960s, as multinational companies began to relocate production in the Far East (and from North to South and Central America), left workers needing to adapt to a new employment landscape, in which educational qualifications and technical skills were at a premium. Those who lacked these were often left with low-paid, insecure, part-time employment or self-employment; more women had entered the labour market, but mainly as secondary contributors to household incomes.

The working class no longer presented a united front; ever since the collapse of the miners' strike in the mid-1970s, the trades union movement represented only a minority of workers. The Labour Party under Tony Blair had become an even more enthusiastic promoter of programmes of privatisation of the public sector than Margaret Thatcher had been, and the eventual transformation of tax credits into Universal Credit under David Cameron institutionalised a divisive scheme which further weakened class solidarity.

Eventually, the decades of de-industrialisation and increasing inequality in the UK provoked demonstrations and marches, in which young people with few prospects of jobs to match their qualifications took to the streets to protest. As had happened in previous demonstrations, the police perceived peaceful demonstrations as 'unruly' and potentially violent, and attempted to disperse them, enabling the militants looking for a fight to hit back in 'self-defence' (BBC Radio 4, 'How Peaceful Protests Turn into Riots', 'The Life Scientific' (presented by Jim Al-Khalili), 16 June, 2020).

The reality of rising debt with few prospects for better work and earning opportunities meant that frustration could at any time turn to anger and mass action. The police were increasingly seen as enemies of the working class, creating an atmosphere of tension in deprived districts.

So the coronavirus pandemic struck an economy in which the income of the working class had been stagnating for almost four decades, as capital gained an ever-larger share of GDP. It caused massive lay-offs and declines in incomes, but it also gave rise to the furlough payments which offered a glimpse of a possible future. If wages would need subsidisation on an even larger scale than before the pandemic, perhaps this could be done according to a principle more consistent with class solidarity. This will be the topic of the next chapter.

References

Beveridge, W. (1942). *Social Insurance and Allied Services*, Cmd 6404. London: HMSO (1966).

Beveridge, W. (1944). *Full Employment in a Free Society*. London: Allen and Unwin.

Dangerfield, G. (1935). *The Strange Death of Liberal England*. London: McGibbon and Kee (1966).

Finer, S. E. (1952). *The Life and Times of Sir Edwin Chadwick*. London: Methuen.

Hay, J. R. (1975). *The Origins of the Liberal Welfare Reforms, 1906–1914*. London: Macmillan.

Keynes, J. M. (1936). *The General Theory of Employment, Interest and Money*. Macmillan (1957).

Spencer, H. (1860). *The Social Organism*. London: Penguin.

Spencer, H. (1884). *The Man* Versus *the State*. London: Penguin.

CHAPTER 8

Unconditional Welfare: The Universal Basic Income

Abstract It might seem clear from previous chapters that there are direct ways in which well-being, and hence social value, can be increased through public policy. One obvious way would be for greater equality of incomes to be sought through fairer distribution. But, as I have argued (pp. 59–60), the institutions for redistribution, especially in the Anglophone countries, have become part of the problem, because they divide the working class, and coerce those who claim means-tested income subsidies. A radical new approach is explored in this chapter.

Keywords Basic Income • Universalism • Poverty • Employment

The pandemic accelerated institutional changes which were already under way. Some of these were fairly trivial, concerned with consumption behaviour, such as more online shopping and less long-distance business travel. But more were derived from the experience that many face-to-face interactions are now unnecessary in an age of digital communications. Education was an obvious example: online teaching and learning proved relatively easy. In health care, non-clinicians were enabled to do routine diagnoses and treatments, saving visits to doctors; in legal disputes, courts and tribunals could conduct remote hearings through video links (BBC Radio 4, 'Rethink: Fast Forward', [presented by Eric Schmidt], 23 June, 2020).

B. Jordan, *Social Value in Public Policy*,
https://doi.org/10.1007/978-3-030-60421-9_8

But another focus was income maintenance. The coronavirus pandemic has revived interest in this issue, because of the massive numbers of citizens who have required state support during social isolation in lock-down, and the selective suspension of much economic activity. This has partly been a simple issue of the fall in national income – a recession – which affected even the very rich. It emerged that a tiny group of these in the UK had lost £54 billion among them in the spring of 2020 (BBC Radio 4, 'News', 17 May, 2020).

But the great majority of those furloughed by their employers, and those with very small businesses, had to rely on claims from state funds, which many of them had not done before. The former – seven and a half million by 16 May (BBC Radio 4, 'Moneybox', presented by Paul Lewis) – were entitled to 80 per cent of their earnings, up to £2500 per month. But employers, who received these funds, were in many cases not paying them. Furthermore, the rules surrounding these measures forbade workers to do any tasks for these employers, but not to work for other firms, or do voluntary work. The tax authorities (HMRC) said that they reserved the right to conduct retrospective audits, to name and shame firms, or even report them for criminal fraud; they said they had already received 795 reports of fraudulent activities or omissions. Furloughed workers could do voluntary work only in the community for the common good, or for the sake of their own health.

All this was superimposed upon the travails of Universal Credit. The attempt to consolidate the several means-tested systems of income maintenance which had been created since the early 1970s had already encountered a series of problems in the ten years since it had begun, and was due to take another four. Now the numbers claiming it were greatly increased (by a million in two weeks in early April, ten times the usual number), causing further administrative difficulties.

There were delays of up to eight hours on the telephone as callers were required to supply identification, and many needed advance payments, made as loans against their eventual entitlements; 10,000 extra staff had been engaged (BBC Radio 4, 'News', 2 April, 2020). New claimants were told that they should submit evidence of spending 35 hours a week seeking employment; if they found part-time work, they were still required to come to the employment office to report their earnings, so that deductions in payments could be made (BBC 2 TV, 'Universal Credit: Inside the System', 11 February, 2020).

The five million self-employed were an especially difficult category, since they were not entitled to benefits arising from unemployment, and could therefore not be categorised as 'furloughed'. In the event, they were quickly included in payments, as eligibility for UC was widened, and waiting time abolished (BBC Radio 4, 'Today', 12 March, 2020). But there were many reports of delays, both in contacting the offices and in receiving payments; the dates when employees were in work to be eligible were also quite arbitrary, and reports of adverse effects on mental health and increased suicide rates were common (BBC Radio 4, 'Moneybox', presented by Paul Lewis, 8 April, 2020).

By mid-June the unemployment rate had not risen, but government statistics showed a 600,000 fall in employees on payrolls and a very large reduction in hours worked (BBC Radio 4, 'News', 16 June, 2020). Young people were most adversely affected, with areas of material deprivation closely correlated with those experiencing the worst health outcomes (BBC Radio 4, 'World at One', presented by Sarah Montague, on the same day).

In the USA, the situation was more straightforward, since President Trump had surprisingly declared himself in favour of unconditional payments to all citizens. The Democratic Party representatives in Congress opposed this, and wanted payments to be means-tested, but the limit eventually imposed was quite permissive, with only those earning $75,000 a year or more being excluded from payments of $1200 a month to every adult and $500 for each child (BBC Radio 4, 'News', 25 March, 2020).

This was not an entire innovation in US social policy. Some 40 years earlier, the windfall discovery of oil reserves in the hitherto undeveloped state of Alaska allowed the Republican governor, Jay Hammond, to fund a range of public services. When there was still a surplus from the tax receipts, his administration decided to pay a dividend to each citizen from an 'Alaska Permanent Fund'. Although the sum (initially $1000 a month) was modest for the oil company employees, it was life-changing for the Native American and Inuit populations of the state.

So the implementation of the idea of universal, unconditional benefits in the Republican-led USA, which had also been adopted in other countries with windfall mineral wealth (Namibia and Mongolia) and in Kerala, India, was not associated with radical politics, even though in the UK and Europe it was advocated by Green Parties. It began to be seen as a serious social policy measure, which received a sudden spurt of attention during the coronavirus pandemic, when neither Continental Social Insurance schemes nor the UK's means-tested Universal Credit was an adequate response to the extent of need.

There was a rash of publications and programmes in the media about the proposal, in *The Times*, the *Daily Mail* and the *Independent* as well as the *New Statesman* and the *Guardian* (see pp. 00–00). The most frequent criticism of the idea – that people would be less motivated to work and earn if they were guaranteed an adequate income – had little relevance while people were furloughed during the pandemic. But the question which now arises is whether the economic recession which inevitably follows the lock-down provides an opportunity for its permanent adoption.

The evidence from the pilot studies, not only in Alaska and the developing countries (Namibia and Mongolia) where windfall mineral wealth for the immigrant few allowed redistribution to the indigenous many, but also in Finland and the European cities where pilot studies were conducted, has been that there was little significant withdrawal from the labour market, except by some women with children, but more importantly, in the most-researched of these, Namibia, women's status improved, children's school attendance rose markedly, use of medical clinics and the number of HIV patients taking medication increased, crime rates fell and income inequalities reduced (interview with Guy Standing, *Citizens Income Newsletter*, 2012, p. 5).

So the obvious conclusion is that it is worth persisting with any moves towards an unconditional UBI which are taken during the pandemic, and introducing it where these have not been conducted. The great advantage of an unconditional income maintenance system is that it makes coercion (workfare, welfare-to-work and the threat of benefits sanctions) irrelevant, since people have a choice about how much time to spend in paid work, and how much in unpaid (but often more satisfying and productive of social value) activities.

More recently, the UBI has begun to be trialled in several European and UK cities, as well as in districts of California (under the enthusiastic sponsorship of Elon Musk). But there now seems to be a wave of support for and adoption of schemes across the USA. The Chief Executive of Twitter, Jack Dorsey, has announced that he is donating $3 million to a number of pilot schemes in 16 cities all over the country. He said that he recognised it as a valuable 'tool to close the wealth and income gap', and that the proposal had gained momentum as a response to the threat to jobs of Artificial Intelligence. He was attracted by the principle of automatic payment irrespective of wealth and employment status (BBC Online,

'News (technology)', 'Twitter boss donates $3 m to Basic Universal Income Project', by Jane Wakefield, technology reporter).

This represented a breakthrough, both because of Dorsey's position in an iconic AI and tech company, and because of its timing, with the US afflicted by the Covid-19 pandemic, and open to new measures to counter economic insecurity and recession. The coalition of city bosses 'Mayors for a Guaranteed Income' had declared itself in favour of the measure because the pandemic had exposed the fragility of most American households and 'disproportionately affected black and brown people', said Dorsey. The mayors had come together to build 'a resilient, just America', and the UBI addressed the 'systematic race and gender inequalities' and created economic security for families (ibid.).

The long-term investment in such projects in US cities as a response to the threat to jobs from new technology is really significant; the burst of interest in it during the pandemic is less surprising. It is now well-positioned to be an important feature of a post-pandemic world.

Conclusions

As this world emerges, it becomes clear that the alternatives of authoritarianism and a more free society, in which the coercion of poor people has been abolished, are at last becoming the potential issues for debate and political contest. A shift in this direction has already occurred in Germany, where the far-right *Alternative für Deutschland* and the Green Party have become the main contenders for power.

If it is accepted that inequality and coercion are two of the main factors in the stagnation of rates of well-being and social value in societies in the past 40 years (Jordan 2008), the recession due to the pandemic will be compensated in the medium term by these new factors. There should also be benefits for relationships among citizens from the mutuality and co-operation that occurred during the pandemic – just as there were in the UK from the solidarity engendered by the sufferings of the Blitz during the Second World War, which was a major factor in the support for the construction of the welfare state in the post-war years.

This was a remarkable achievement, given how stuck in a conservative, class-ridden culture the society had been in the 1930s, and how little governments had done in that decade to relieve the distress of the people, or to reform obviously inadequate institutions. The war on the coronavirus may be our equivalent of the struggle against Nazism in those times.

Another challenge will be the future path of automation, especially in service work (Jordan 2020). Artificial intelligence is already capable of most of the tasks human beings can perform, both physical and intellectual. Algorithms can replicate human abilities to make plans and execute them, increasingly approaching the moment when robots can think for themselves.

In an analysis of the issues raised by these potential developments, Helen Lewis (BBC Radio 4, 'The Spark', 16 May, 2020) interviewed ethical philosophers about these dilemmas. Human designers could ensure that machines are designed to satisfy only human preferences, but this will require tight regulation of firms such as those in Silicon Valley which are highly resistant to such controls.

The dilemmas of politics in an age when machines are more intelligent than people were foreseen by E.M. Forster in his story 'The Machine Stops' (1909). Having lost the capacity to live on the earth's surface, human individuals survive in cells below ground, isolated from each other, but with all their needs (physical and intellectual) met by an omnipotent Machine; they communicate with each other by a kind of internet. Eventually, humans come to worship the Machine, forgetting that they created it, and how to control it. When it breaks down, they perish.

The present situation is not apocalyptic, but our future relationship with technology does pose vital dilemmas and challenges. These will be analysed in the concluding chapter.

References

Forster, E. M. (1909, November). The Machine Stops. *Oxford and Cambridge Review*.

Jordan, B. (2008). *Welfare and Well-Being: Social Value in Public Policy*. Bristol: Policy Press.

Jordan, B. (2020). *Automation and Human Solidarity*. Basingstoke: Palgrave Macmillan.

CHAPTER 9

Conclusions

Abstract This book has explored an idea which has suddenly entered the field of public policy in this decade. When I wrote *Welfare and Well-being: Social Value in Public Policy* (2008), it had not been used since Schumpeter's *The Nature and Essence of Economic Theory*, 1908 (Trans. Bruce McDaniel. New Brunswick: Transaction Publishers (2010)), and then only to denote the value of collective goods. But the significance of social value in public policy has increased sharply during the coronavirus crisis, because of the polarisation in political responses to the pandemic and the economic recession it brought about, which seems certain to ensue as we emerge from lock-down.

Keywords Globalisation • Nationalism • War • Recovery

The strong temptation for political movements everywhere will be to try to restore an approach to economic growth which is technical and consensual (Gray 2020), in an effort to conserve some of the 'wartime spirit' which prevailed during the crisis. But I have argued in this book that underlying divisions and conflicts of interest in societies cannot be so easily laid aside, and that radical new measures are needed if they are not to bring about a decisive turn away from the values and rights of liberal democracy.

B. Jordan, *Social Value in Public Policy*,
https://doi.org/10.1007/978-3-030-60421-9_9

The path to a pursuit of well-being and social value is not obvious or straightforward. The clearest case for it lies in the alternatives – authoritarianism, growing inequality and the growth of coercive social policies, in combination making up a political culture full of tensions, conflicts and restrictions. A politics of well-being and social value could counter all of these, but not always in obvious ways.

For instance, the approach to income maintenance through an unconditional Universal Basic Income would be expensive, but not the most redistributive option available, because the better-off would also be beneficiaries; it could alleviate inequalities only when combined with a progressive income tax system. Its greatest relevance to the immediate future lies in creating common interests among the whole population, and minimising the coercion of poorer citizens.

But other, quite different, issues illustrate the kinds of dilemmas which will arise. Because the divisive effects of the long stagnation in the real value of wages had fed into the Brexit vote, especially in the North of England, and strongly influenced the outcome of the December, 2019, General Election, an Immigration Bill to address the new situation was due to be debated in Parliament soon after the strictest phase of the lockdown was lifted. This placed a floor on the wages of anyone wishing to enter the UK for employment.

But this restrictive approach was challenged when the Chinese government clamped down violently on pro-democracy demonstrations in Hong Kong, and enacted powers to arrest and deport the leaders of the movement. The UK's administration felt obliged to offer asylum to some 3 million Hong Kong citizens with British passports, allowing them to enter the country and qualify for citizenship after six years. Even though there was evidence that many would not avail themselves of this opportunity because of family and community ties (BBC World Service, 'From Our Own Correspondent', 12 July, 2020), this would represent a dramatic change of direction in immigration policy.

Opposition MPs had already pointed out that the new measure excluded many NHS auxiliary workers and cleaners, and nearly all the immigrant staff of care homes – the heroes of the recent pandemic, and themselves disproportionately among the victims. The government's plan to train new recruits from school and university leavers was obviously unrealistic – almost as unconvincing as the idea that these same young British citizens would make up the shortfall in fruit-pickers that would be another category of those hit by immigration restrictions (BBC Radio 4, 'Yesterday in Parliament', 19 May, 2020).

The other side of the same coin was that this generation of young British citizens were unlikely to have the same range of options for moving between more suitable work experiences, as a pathway towards rewarding and fulfilling careers. There was evidence (confirmed by both Paul Johnson of the Institute for Fiscal Studies and Thorsten Bell of the Resolution Foundation) that the loss of such opportunities affected the momentum and upward trajectory of this cohort, and would scar their earnings and promotion prospects for the rest of their working live (BBC Radio 4, 'Today', 19 May, 2020).

At the other end of the institutional scale, the German Constitutional Court was at odds with the European Central Bank over the extent of monetary easing in the face of the recession. The court accused the Bank of undermining confidence in the euro and 'killing off any hope of euro-bonds or joint debt insurance', as well as breaching EU treaty law. It accused the Bank of having 'manifestly' breached the principle of proportionality with mass bond purchases (of over 2.2 trillion euros and expected to rise further) and having trespassed from monetary to broad economic policy-making ('Germany's Top Court Clashes with European Central Bank in Revolutionary Ruling', by Ambrose Evans Pritchard, *The Telegraph* website, 5 May, 2020).

So at every level, from the experiences of young people in the UK to the relations between one of the highest courts in Continental Europe and the EU's Central Bank, there was hopelessness, confusion and conflict in the wake of the pandemic. This concluding chapter will explore the possible way forward in the face of these challenges.

The Role of the UK in the Global Economy

Previous crises for the UK in the twenty-first century centred on the financial sector. With the decline of the manufacturing industry from the 1960s, and the growth of services which reflected inequalities of income (low-paid work to meet the needs of the wealthy minority), it was the banks and insurance companies concentrated in the City of London which took on disproportionate importance, as the only part of the national economy with conspicuous success worldwide, yet also a sector very vulnerable to global shocks. But the pandemic was a shock of a different kind, with the greatest impact on face-to-face services, ethnic minorities and poor communities.

If this crisis resembled any previous one, it was perhaps that which overtook the Macmillan government in the early 1960s. Although this is remembered most vividly for the Christine Keeler scandal, over a Cabinet Minister's involvement with a high-class prostitute, the underlying issues which came to the surface then were issues over the country's future global role. With the independence of so many of the former Empire countries in Africa during the previous decade (what Macmillan called the 'Wind of Change'), there was a vacuum which became obvious, because the overture by the Prime Minister and his envoy, Edward Heath, towards General de Gaulle over membership of the European Community had been suddenly rebuffed.

If Macmillan lost his way at this point in his leadership, a more changeable and inconsistent figure still was Enoch Powell. A brigadier at age 24 during the war, he quickly rose to Cabinet office as a supporter of the British Empire, but then became a Nationalist in the 1960s, and made his notorious speech about the 'Rivers of Blood' which would flow if Commonwealth immigration was not checked in 1968, quoting the example of the race riots then taking place in the USA. Having supported Britain's earlier attempt to join the European Common Market, he opposed membership in the 1970s, and became anti-American as well (Edgerton 2019, pp. 260–1).

In the new century, the UK's global role is confused and unclear. Because of the legacy of Empire and the links embodied in the Commonwealth, there are many British citizens living on every continent. Economic globalisation has meant that British firms have branches and outlets which are similarly widespread, and the UK's economy is very dependent on imports for components of its high-tech products, as has become clear in various circumstances, from storms to strikes, when supply chains were interrupted.

But the most controversial issues have concerned British involvement in military operations, such as the long war in Afghanistan, and in the conflicts in Kosovo and Sierra Leone, both at the turn of the twenty-first century. By far the most significant of these was the decision to join the USA in an invasion of Iraq in 2003, justified by Prime Minister Blair by reference to the Nazi threat of the 1930s and to Saddam Hussein's possession of 'Weapons of Mass Destruction' (no evidence of which was later discovered).

This was an instance of the UK trying to retain a significant role in global politics through its close relationship with the USA. The enduring image of Blair and President George W. Bush marching in lock-step, in a kind of parody of military might, symbolised this weakness posing as strength. The rationalisations and untruths used to justify these actions had the reverse effect, of revealing the UK's dependence and enfeeblement (Edgerton 2019, pp. 515–7).

Final Thoughts

Well-being and social value will therefore have to compete with several other priorities and policies, including military prestige, Imperial nostalgia, dependence on the USA, the global interests of international companies, inequalities of income and coercive benefits systems, in order to become central to public policies in the UK. They will face different but substantial obstacles elsewhere. There are very few Bhutans in the world – benevolent Buddhist monarchies, which can introduce such principles as priorities for their citizens by edict.

But the coronavirus pandemic has supplied a break in the flow of economic and political forces which has involved, as I have shown, some surprising developments, such as those in the USA (see pp. 66–7). The power and effectiveness of national state agencies, the self-sacrifice of public servants, the voluntary commitment of millions of ordinary people, and the everyday willingness of most to endure hardships without complaint have all suggested that many of the least attractive features of consumerist and competitive cultures are only skin-deep. People are potentially better (more public-spirited and co-operative) than the marketing managers have tried to make them, and the shrill media commentators have portrayed them to be.

So it is probably only the threat of climate change that can focus attention on these measures in the medium term. In countries like Australia and India and in the southern states of the USA, extreme weather conditions demand the attention of the international community, and protests by young people will refocus their concerns once the coronavirus pandemic has passed. Then the measures discussed in the later chapters of this book will again start to command political support, with the added credentials of the experiences gained during the pandemic itself.

But there are also danger signs. The misuse of AI is reckoned to cost some $1.3 trillion, yet it has not been deployed to address climate change to any effect so far. Some fear that it could initiate changes with unintended consequences, such as using up all the earth's oxygen or water supply, or making everyone sterile. People could be made more malleable and easily satisfied; the ethical issues are vast and quite difficult to anticipate (BBC Radio 4, 'The Spark', presented by Helen Lewis, 18 May, 2020).

In this book, I have argued that the greatest limitation on well-being and social value in the Western developed countries has been the inequality that accompanied capitalist globalisation in recent decades. But two new factors are now added to this one. First, the coronavirus pandemic is of unknown duration, and could continue to afflict many nations worldwide. Second, the ambitions of China, based on a combination of authoritarianism, technology and consumerism, are driving a new wave of globalisation, which poses a threat to liberty and human rights across large parts of Asia and Africa. Social value as a criterion for the future evolution of human societies faces an uphill struggle.

References

Edgerton, D. (2019). *The Rise and Fall of the British Nation: A Twentieth-Century History*. London: Penguin.

Gray, J. (2020, July 10–16). State of the Nation: In an Age of Disorder, the Fundamental Challenge Is to Retain a Fragile Peace in a Culture of Fragments. *New Statesman*, 23–26.

Jordan, B. (2008). *Welfare and Well-Being: Social Value in Public Policy*. Bristol: Policy Press.

Schumpeter, J. (1908). *The Nature and Essence of Economic Theory*. Trans. Bruce McDaniel. New Brunswick: Transaction Publishers (2010).

References

Austen, J. (1813). *Pride and Prejudice*. London: Penguin (1965).

Austen, J. (1814). *Mansfield Park*. London: Penguin (1966).

Bache, I., & Reardon, L. (2016). *The Policy and Politics of Well-Being: Understanding the Rise and Significance of a New Agenda*. Cheltenham: Edward Elgar.

Bache, I., & Scott, K. (Eds). (2018). *The Politics of Well-Being: Theory, Policy and Practice*. Basingstoke: Palgrave Macmillan.

Barry, B. (1997). The Attractions of Basic Income. In J. Franklin (Ed.), *Equality* (pp. 157–171). London: Institute for Public Policy Research.

Becker, H. S. (1974). Labelling Theory Reconsidered. In His *Outsiders*. New York: Free Press.

Behan, B. (1958). *Borstal Boy*. Dublin: Arena Books.

Benstead, S. (2020, March 19). The Universal Basic Income: What Is It, How Does It Work, and Could It Help the Coronavirus Crisis? *Daily Telegraph*.

Bentham, J. (1791). Panopticon, or the Inspection House. In J. Bowring (Ed.), *The Works of Jeremy Bentham in 11 Volumes* (Vol. 4). Edinburgh: Tait.

Beveridge, Sir W. (1942). *Social Insurance and Allied Services*, Cm 6804. London: HMSO.

Beveridge, Sir W. (1944). *Full Employment in a Free Society*. London: Methuen.

Brown, A. (2020, April 22). Britain Can Move Towards a Universal Basic Income – Just Look at Spain. *The Sun*.

Buchanan, J. M. (1968). *The Demand and Supply of Public Goods*. New York: Rand McNally.

Challis, D., & Davies, B. (1985). *The Long-term Care of the Elderly: The Community Care Scheme*. Discussion Paper 386. Canterbury: Personal Social Research Unit, University of Kent.

B. Jordan, *Social Value in Public Policy*,
https://doi.org/10.1007/978-3-030-60421-9

Cobb, M. (2020). *The Idea of the Brain: A History*. London: Profile Books.
Dangerfield, G. (1935). *The Strange Death of Liberal England*. London: McGibbon and Kee (1966).
Deeming, C. (2013). Addressing the Determinants of Subjective Well-Being: The Latest Challenge for Social Policy. *Journal of Social Policy, 42*(3), 541–565.
Deeming, C., & Hayes, D. (2012). Worlds of Welfare Capitalism and Well-Being: A Multilevel Analysis. *Journal of Social Policy, 41*(4), 811–829.
Deeming, C., & Jones, K. (2015). Investigating the Macro-determinants of Self-Rated Health and Well-Being Using the European Survey: Methodological Innovations Across Countries and Time. *International Journal of Sociology, 45*(4), 256–285.
Department of Health. (1989). *Caring for People: Community Care in the Next Decade and Beyond*. London: Department of Health/HMSO.
Department of Health. (1998). *Modernising Social Services: Promoting Independence, Improving Protection, Raising Standards*, Cm 4169. London: Department of Health/HMSO.
Dickens, C. (1837–8). *Oliver Twist*. London: Chapman and Hall (1911).
Dickens, C. (1852–3). *Bleak House*. London: Chapman and Hall (1911).
Dilnot Commission. (2011). *Fairer Funding for All: Report of the Commission on Funding for Care and Support*. London: Department of Health.
Drakeford, M. (2006). Ownership, Regulation and Public Interest. *Critical Social Policy, 26*(4), 932–944.
Edgerton, D. (2019). *The Rise and Fall of the British Nation: A Twentieth-Century History*. London: Penguin.
Ermisch, J. (1985). *The Political Economy of Demographic Change*. London: Heinemann.
Feinstein, C. H. (1976). *Statistical Tables of National Income, Expenditure and Output of the UK, 1855–1965*. Cambridge: Cambridge University Press.
Fielding, H. (1749). *Tom Jones, A Foundling*. London: Penguin Classics (1980).
Finch, J., & Groves, D. (1984). *Labour of Love*. London: Allen and Unwin.
Finer, S. E. (1952). *The Life and Times of Sir Edwin Chadwick*. London: Methuen.
Forster, E. M. (1909, November). The Machine Stops. *Oxford and Cambridge Review*.
Foucault, M. (1975). Discipline and Punish. In P. Rabinow (Ed.), *The Foucault Reader; An Introduction to Foucault's Thought*. London: Penguin (1981).
Freud, S. (1929). Civilisation and Its Discontents. In *Civilisation, War and Death: Psycho-analytical Epitomes*, No. 4. London: Hogarth Press (1935).
Gershuny, J. I. (1983). *Social Innovation and the Division of Labour*. Oxford: Oxford University Press.
GMB. (2011, October 4). *Four Seasons Healthcare Accounts for 2010: How Earnings (EBITARM) of £8408 Per Resident Per Annum to Pay Interest on £79 Million Loans and Rents*.

Goffman, E. (1967). On Face Work: An Analysis of Ritual Elements in Interaction. In *Interaction Ritual: Essays in Face-to-Face Behaviour* (pp. 1–46). New York: Doubleday Anchor.

Haagh, L. (2019). Public Ownership with Varieties of Capitalism: Regulatory Foundations for Welfare and Freedom. *International Journal of public Policy, 15*(1/2), 153–184.

Hardy, T. (1894). *Jude the Obscure*. London: Macmillan.

Hay, J. R. (1975). *The Origins of the Liberal Reforms, 1906–14*. London: Macmillan.

Helliwell, J. F. (2003). How's Life? Comparing Individual and National Variables to Explain Subjective Well-Being. *Economic Modelling, 29*, 331–360.

Hines, B. (1968). *A Kestrel for a Knave*. London: Penguin.

House of Commons Public Accounts Committee. (2011, December 6). *Report on the Enquiry into the Southern Cross Care Company*.

Institute of Government. (2019). *Adult Social Care*. London: Institute of Government Performance Tracker.

Johnson, J., Rolf, S., & Smith, R. (2010). Uncovering History: Private Care Homes for Older People in England. *Journal of Social Policy, 39*(2), 235–253.

Jordan, B. (1973). *Paupers: The Making of the New Claiming Class*. London: Routledge and Kegan Paul.

Jordan, B. (1976). *Freedom and the Welfare State*. London: Routledge and Kegan Paul (Republished 2019).

Jordan, B. (1986). *The Common Good: Citizenship, Morality and Self-Interest*. Oxford: Blackwell.

Jordan, B. (1987). *Rethinking Welfare*. Oxford: Blackwell.

Jordan, B. (1996). *A Theory of Poverty and Social Exclusion*. Cambridge: Polity.

Jordan, B. (2006). *Social Policy for the Twenty-First Century: New Perspectives, Big Issues*. Cambridge: Polity.

Jordan, B. (2007a). *Social Work and Well-Being*. Lyme Regis: Russell House Publishers.

Jordan, B. (2007b). Social Value in Policies for Children. *Journal of Children's Services, 4*, 51–66.

Jordan, B. (2008). *Welfare and Well-Being: Social Value in Public Value*. Bristol: Policy Press.

Jordan, B. (2010a). *Why the Third Way Failed: Economics, Morality and the Origins of the 'Big Society'*. Bristol: Policy Press.

Jordan, B. (2010b). *What's Wrong with Social Policy and How to Fix It*. Cambridge: Polity.

Jordan, B. (2019). *Authoritarianism and How to Counter It*. London: Palgrave.

Jordan, B. (2020). *Automation and Human Solidarity*. London: Palgrave.

Jordan, B., & Drakeford, M. (2012). *Social Work and Social Policy Under Austerity*. Basingstoke: Macmillan.

Jordan, B., James, S., Redley, M., & Kay, H. (1992). *Trapped in Poverty?: Labour-Market Decisions with Low Income Households*. London: Routledge.
Jordan, B., Redley, M., & James, S. (1994). *Putting the Family First: Identities, Decisions, Citizenship*. London: UCL Press.
Kahneman, D. (1999). Objective Well-Being. In D. Kahneman, E. Diener, & N. Schwartz (Eds.), *The Foundations of Hedonic Psychology*. New York: Russell Sage Foundation.
Keynes, J. M. (1936). *A General Theory of Employment, Interest and Money*. London: Macmillan.
Lawrence, D. H. (1914). *Sons and Lovers*. London: Penguin (1974).
Layard, R. (2005). *Happiness: Lessons from a New Science*. London: Allen Lane.
Marcuse, H. (1969). *An Essay in Liberation*. London: Penguin (1984).
Macfarlane, A. (1976). *The Origins of English Individualism: The Family, Property and Social Transition*. Oxford: Blackwell.
Marx, K. (1877). *Capital: A Critique of Political Economy*. London: Penguin.
Miller, E. J., & Gwynne, G. V. (1972). *A Life Apart: A Pilot Study of Residential Institutions for Boys*. London: Tavistock Publications.
Oates, W. E. (1972). *Fiscal Federalism*. New York: Harcourt Brace Jovanovitch.
Offe, C. (1992). A Non-Productivist Design for Social Policies. In P. Van Parijs (Ed.), *Arguing for Basic Income: Ethical Foundations for a Radical Reform* (pp. 161–186). London: Verso.
Office of Population Censuses and Surveys. (1983). *General Household Survey, 1983*. London: HMSO.
Olson, M. (1965). *The Logic of Collective Action: Public Goods and the Theory of Groups*. Cambridge, MA: Harvard University Press.
Olson, M. (1982). *The Rise and Decline of Nations: Economic Growth, Stagflation and Social Rigidities*. New Haven: Yale University Press.
Pahl, R. E. (1984). *Divisions of Labour*. Oxford: Blackwell.
Parker, H. (1989). *Instead of the Dole: An Enquiry into the Integration of the Tax and Benefit System*. London: Routledge.
Purdy, D. (1995). Citizenship, Basic Income and the State. *New Left Review, 208*, 427–439.
Ricardo, D. (1817). *Principles of Political Economy and Taxation*. Edinburgh: Dent (1912).
Schumpeter, J. (1908). *The Nature and Essence of Economic Theory*. Trans. Bruce McDaniel. New Brunswick: Transaction Publishers (2010).
Scourfield, P. (2007). Are There Reasons to Be Worried About the 'Cartellisation' of Residential Care? *Critical Social Policy, 25*(2), 255–280.
Sillitoe, A. (1958). *Saturday Night and Sunday Morning*. London: W.H. Allen.
Smith, A. (1759). *The Theory of Moral Sentiments* (pp. 7–280). New York: Harper Row (1948).

Smith, A. (1776). *An Inquiry Concerning the Nature and Causes of the Wealth of Nations.* Oxford: Clarendon Press (1976).
Spencer, H. (1860). *The Social Organism.* London: Penguin.
Spencer, H. (1884). *The Man* Versus *the State.* London: Penguin.
Standing, G. (2011). *The Precariat; The New Dangerous Class.* London: Bloomsbury.
Standing, G. (2017). *The Corruption of Capitalism: Why* Rentiers *Thrive and Work Does Not Pay.* London: Biteback.
Stone, J. (2020, April 27). Public Support Universal Basic Income, Job Guarantee and Rent Controls to Respond to Coronavirus, Poll Finds. *The Independent.*
Thin, N. (2012). *Social Happiness: Theory into Policy and Practice.* Bristol: Policy Press.
Tolstoy, L. (1874–6). *War and Peace.* London: Penguin Classics (1979).
Van Parijs, P. (1995). *Real Freedom for All: What (If Anything) Can Justify Capitalism?* Oxford: Clarendon Press.
Wallace, J., & Schmuekler, K. (2012). *Shifting the Dial: From Well-Being Measurement to Policy Practice.* Dunfermline: Carnegie UK Trust/Institute for Public Policy Research.
Walmsley, A., & de Sousa, E. (2010). *Philosophies of Science.* Paper Presented at a Conference 'Theory and Philosophy'. Blackwater Castle, 3rd April.
White, S., & Jha, S. (2018). Towards an Interdisciplinary Approach to Well-Being: Life Histories and Self-Determining Theory in Rural Zambia. *Social Science and Medicine, 212*, 153–166.
Wilkinson, R., & Pickett, K. (2009). *The Spirit Level: Why More Equal Societies Almost Always Do Better.* London: Allen Lane.
Wren Lewis, S. (2019). *The Happiness Problem: Expecting Better in an Uncertain World.* Bristol: Policy Press.
Young, J. (1971). *The Drug-Takers: The Social Meaning of Drug Use.* London: Paladin.
Zuboff, S. (2019). *The Age of Surveillance Capitalism and the Fight for a Human Future at the Frontier of Power.* New York: Profile Book.

Index

B. Jordan, *Social Value in Public Policy*,
https://doi.org/10.1007/978-3-030-60421-9

Milton Keynes UK
Ingram Content Group UK Ltd.
UKHW030100141223
434262UK00005B/40

9 783030 604202